IntechOpen

Family Therapy - New Intervention Programs and Researches

Edited by Floriana Irtelli

Published in London, United Kingdom

Supporting open minds since 2005

Family Therapy - New Intervention Programs and Researches
http://dx.doi.org/10.5772/intechopen.81558
Edited by Floriana Irtelli

Contributors
David Allen, Keva Bethell, Marie Allen-Carroll, Flavia D'Alessandro, Katherine Stavrianopoulos, Hamilton Wagner, Tania Madureira Dalallana, Silvia Lordello, Eva Mydlíková, Klaus Henner Spierling, Kirsty Tatah-Wraith, Helena Kulikowska, Dympna Cunnane, Hassan Karimi, Fred Piercy, Tina Savla, Barbara Cordella, Paola Elia, Alessia Carleschi, Marzia Pibiri

First published in London, United Kingdom, 2019 by IntechOpen
IntechOpen is the global imprint of INTECHOPEN LIMITED, registered in England and Wales, registration number: 11086078, The Shard, 25th floor, 32 London Bridge Street
London, SE19SG - United Kingdom
Printed in Croatia

British Library Cataloguing-in-Publication Data
A catalogue record for this book is available from the British Library

Additional hard and PDF copies can be obtained from orders@intechopen.com

Family Therapy - New Intervention Programs and Researches
Edited by Floriana Irtelli
p. cm.
Print ISBN 978-1-78984-301-9
Online ISBN 978-1-78984-302-6
eBook (PDF) ISBN 978-1-83962-191-8

Meet the editor

Floriana Irtelli, psychoanalyst and psychotherapist, member of the Italian Society of the Psychoanalysis of Relationships, has been lecturing for several years at the Catholic University of the Sacred Heart, Milan, Italy. She has worked at the Fatebenefratelli Hospital, Milan, performing scientific research and clinical activities. She is among the authors of books such as *A Fresh Look at Anxiety Disorders* and *Psychopathy—New Updates on an Old Phenomenon*, and has published articles for the *Journal of Affective Disorders*, *Journal of Research in Psychotherapy*, and *Journal of Psychiatric and Mental Health Nursing*. She has participated in numerous conferences, seminars, and congresses, such as the 2015 World Congress of Psycho-Oncology. She is also the author *Illuminarsi di Ben-essere*, *Familiar-mente*, and *Contemporary Perspectives on Relational Wellness, Psychoanalysis and the Modern Family*. She is the editor of *Psychosis, Biopsychosocial and Relational Perspectives*.

Contents

Preface

We can say that at first glance in the works of Freud, psychoanalysis would seem to be a theory of the individual, but it is reckoned that these theoretical elaborations also contain a latent family-group dimension; in fact, even if psychoanalysis originated as a method of treatment of individuals, and Freud elaborated most of the theories in terms of "intrapsychic structures," we must not forget that it was psychoanalysis that discovered and signaled that the human being is not conceivable without the existence of others, and that those paradoxical "attempts at care" that make human beings, classified as "symptoms," have a meaning not only for the individual, but also for the relationships with others. The relational theories are therefore salient in psychoanalysis and embrace the family dimension, in continuity with that of the couple: indeed, group, family, and couple are privileged areas of relationship, of bond. The approach to the family and the couple has attracted the attention of psychoanalysts to the importance of the function of intersubjectivity in the genesis and maintenance of the structure of the psyche (and the symptoms) and has opened up new horizons, even on the most "primitive" levels of the psyche, which are expressed also in the context of family sessions. The experience with families allows us to focus on the importance of real and concrete actions within the family ties, leading to a clear evolution and openness to relationships, which allows the possibility for creating new technical conditions to deal with situations in which usually "we do not know how to do with the individual approach" (...). Also, in the *Three Essays on Sexual Theory* (1905), Freud speaks of the possible influence of the parents in the transmission of neuroses to their children [1]. We can therefore affirm that family therapy was born from psychoanalysis; it can in fact be noted that also other authors belonging to the psychoanalysis field that dealt with family relations were Bowlby [2–5] and Winnicott [6–8]. These authors observed that the symptoms of individuals are connected with relationship problems with other people, and later this assumption was also shared and supported by other psychological approaches. Recently, some theoretical developments have brought psychoanalytic thinking even closer to the attention of family therapists and vice versa [1]. It should also be pointed out that over the years, different models of psychotherapy and intervention with the family have been developed and many cannot be defined as psychoanalytic, because they have chosen to focus on different theories, greatly enriching the panorama concerning research, interventions, and therapies for intergenerational and family problems.

The therapeutic intervention approaches are varied, but in all of them it is important to remember the role of the relationship, both in the treatment and in the formation of the same disorder. Psychological care in the family environment aims to create a space in which to reflect together and have new knowledge about oneself and relationships with others, knowing is therefore understood as reflecting. One can reflect on family history, culture, genealogy, and daily interactions that contribute to influencing the person's inner scenario, the various chapters that have been presented help to reflect on many different aspects of family life, offering a very wide, rich, and detailed perspective, with specific insights. In any case, reflecting must always become an opportunity for relational transformation, because the person must be understood as a relational being. Finally, it should be pointed out that in psychological interventions for the family, of any kind, ethics is certainly also important, which is subject to time and culture, and it consists of taking responsibility for one's own actions, reflecting on mistakes, helping the ones in trouble, improving relations, cooperating and sharing. A mixed approach, composed of different perspectives regarding family interventions, certainly offers the best chance to plan these interventions to help those in difficulty in any age group. As a matter of fact, some interesting topics are developed in this book, ranging from the concept of systemic psychotherapy and family therapy to the adoptive born, to daily life in a foster home. Other specific topics of interest are related more specifically to adolescence, childhood, and resocialization.

Floriana Irtelli
Catholic University of the Sacred Heart,
Milan, Italy

Italian Society of Psychoanalysis of the relationship (SIPRe),
Milan, Italy

References

[1] Irtelli F. Contemporary Perspectives on Relational Wellness. Psychoanalysis and the Modern Family. New York: Palgrave McMillan; 2018

[2] Bowlby J. Attachment and Loss. Vol. 1: Attachment. New York: Basic Books; 1969

[3] Bowlby J. Attachment and Loss. Vol. 2: Separation: Anxiety and Anger. New York: Basic Books; 1973

[4] Bowlby J. Attachment and Loss. Vol. 3: Loss: Sadness and Depression. New York: Basic Books; 1980

[5] Bowlby J. A Secure Base. London: Routledge; 1988

[6] Winnicott DW. The theory of the parent-infant relationship. International Journal of Psychoanalysis. 1960 Jan (1):585, London

[7] Winnicott DW. The Family and Individual Development. London: Tavistock; Rome: Armando, 1968; 1965

[8] Winnicott DW. The Maturational Processes and the Facilitating Environment. York: International Universities Press; 1965. Emotional Development and Environment: Studies on the Development of Affect Theory. Rome: Armando; 1977

Section 1

An Overview about Family Therapy

Chapter 1

A Chronological Map of Common Factors across Three Stages of Marriage and Family Therapy

Hassan Karimi, Fred Piercy and Jyoti Savla

Abstract

Meta-analysis research supports the notion that common factors are at work across theoretically different therapies. However, some advocates of empirically supported treatments (ESTs) criticize that there is no common factor chronological map to guide clinicians across different stages of therapy (initial, intermediate, termination). In this chapter, supported by recent research, we propose a preliminary chronological map which has the potential to guide clinicians as they use common factors across all three stages of couple and family therapy. The common factors approach is an overarching therapeutic model within which the therapist can determine and use well-timed common mechanisms of change to support therapy's success. This is consistent with the AAMFT Core Competencies to provide safe and effective therapy.

Keywords: common factors, chronological map, process-research, systemic therapy, family therapy

1. Introduction

Outcome research has supported the therapy effectiveness in psychotherapy and Marriage and Family Therapy (MFT) fields [1]. The findings, over decades of comparative studies, indicate therapy is effective. It can be as effective as medical treatment, and its outcome can last longer than medical treatment [2, 3]. However, the therapy field still deals with controversial debates regarding how therapy provides change and thorough what mechanisms? [4, 5].

In reaction to Hans Eysenck's [6] claim that psychotherapy is ineffective, a series of outcome research studies were conducted that itself caused the emergence of competitive treatment models. Such a trend led in the movement of Empirically Supported Treatments (ESTs) to find the most effective treatments for specific problems [3, 7, 8]. That is, the advocates of ESTs assumed their model-specific factors/techniques were the mechanisms responsible for therapy effectiveness [9]. Therefore, these researchers support outcome research and more controlled comparative studies to establish a specific treatment manual for each specific clinical problem [10]. On the other hand, the advocates of the common factors (CFs) approach believe that shared factors/change mechanisms are responsible for therapeutic outcome across all successful treatment models [3, 8]. They assume that there is not one significant model that achieves higher efficacy than others. For a few decades, we have seen a loop of research between the two camps. The advocates of model specificity piled supportive findings for their models' efficacy, which provided more raw data for advocates of CFs to run meta-analysis that shows equal efficacy across different treatment models [3, 11]. Breaking such a loop toward a better understanding of therapeutic change mechanisms requires more process research and multiple research methods [4, 5, 11]. Process research, by focusing on specific "whats," "whys," "whens," and "hows," can contribute to more clinically relevant and theoretically integrative models.

In this chapter, we provide an overview of the common factors approach and its development. We also discuss the critiques that ESTs advocates posit on CFs approach. Then, we propose a chronological map of when certain common factors are most relevant, which is supported by our qualitative research, as well as other MFT literature. Finally, we discuss the research, clinical, and training implications of the chronological map.

2. Development of common factors approach

Rosenzweig [12] was the first to discuss common factors in the literature. He suggested therapy effectiveness is due to a therapeutic relationship and a treatment rationale that justifies therapeutic tasks. Frank's [13] work prepared the field to move toward integrative therapies. Frank proposed four key dimensions of healing process: (1) an emotionally charged confiding relationship, (2) a therapeutic context, (3) a credible rational that provides a convincing explanation for the client's problem and how to resolve it, and (4) a procedure or task that requires active participation of the client. Then, the research of Luborsky et al. [14] found equivalency of effectiveness across active treatments, which indicated three of every four clients improved, regardless of treatment type.

Lambert [15], based on a review of outcome studies, proposed a four-factors model of what factors contribute to effectiveness, with estimated percentages, including extra-therapeutic change factors 40%, common factors 30%, technique factors 15%, and expectancy factors 15%. Though these percentages were mostly interpreted or cited as factual, empirical evidence, a recent study by Karimi [16] indicates that the percentage of each CFs category can vary due to specific characteristics of therapist, client, problem, etc. That is, the CFs are not a set of static factors, but are dynamic and interactive factors. Another significant contribution by Lambert [15] is a developmental conceptualization of therapy as a process that contains three sequencing stages: support factors, learning factors, and action factors.

A few other insightful theories of integration [17–20] have been introduced in the field, which emphasized mostly common mechanisms/processes of change across treatment models. For example, Goldfried and Padawer [18] conceptualized therapy at three differentiated levels that include: *theories, strategies, and interventions*. At the highest level of abstraction, theories intend to explain human functioning and pathology. At the lowest level of abstraction, techniques which are linked to specific theories intend to generate change. And strategies are within the middle level of abstraction which can be activated by different techniques. It seems that experienced therapists consider these strategies or change processes as a heuristic guide in their practice [21]. For example, the therapists deliberately can choose from seemingly different techniques (e.g., cognitive restructuring, empty chair, family sculpting, paradoxical homework, etc.) when they target a particular change process (e.g., detriangling from parents), which meets the therapy goal (improvement of depression).

Though, the advocates of ESTs insist on manualizing specific protocols for specific problems/disorders [9]. The integrative and CFs scholars [11, 22] challenge the uniformity myths in ESTs, which assumes therapy is consistently applied across therapists and clients. In theory, the therapist may start with a specific model, but in actual practice, the therapist's behavior is mostly guided by the client's responses/characteristics, so the process turns into a progressively individualized one [23, 24]. In addition, the most comprehensive evidence-based study to date (American Psychological Association Task Force, 1993) indicated that there were no differences among all forms of treatment (cognitive behavioral therapy, interpersonal therapy, medication with management, and placebo plus clinical management) on the client's level of depression, but there was a difference in the level of the therapeutic efficacy of the therapists; while the treatment models, the settings, and even the therapist experience were controlled [25].

Sprenkle and Blow [11] proposed a moderate definition of CFs in the marriage and family therapy field; they consider CFs as the main mechanisms of change, though specific models play a role in therapeutic change too. In fact, they consider models as vehicles that delineate a temporal sequence indicating when each CFs should be punctuated during the therapy process. They proposed six categories of common factors: client, therapist, relationship, expectancy/hope, Non-specific mechanisms, unique MFT common factors. Since therapy inherently is a multilevel interactional process [21, 22], such a distinction between the components is more artificial than factual. For the purpose of this chapter, we use this moderate definition of common factors. However, we believe future research may well modify these common factors or introduce new items to improve the conceptualization of CFs.

2.1 Client factors

Client factors include a set of characteristics (e.g., motivation, spirituality and religious faith, cognitive ability, self-agency, cooperation on therapeutic tasks, perseverance, expectations) that are potential resources that relate to clients' movement toward their therapy goal. Unfortunately, professional centrism caused the field to overlook the invaluable therapeutic potency of client factors [8, 26]. Clients usually edit and reconstruct therapeutic interventions and the therapist's style to individualize them to their values and goals. According to Miller and associates [27], "The research literature makes it clear that the client is actually the single most potent contributor to outcome in psychotherapy."

2.2 Therapist factors

Researchers proposed a set of characteristics for therapists (e.g., therapist positivity and friendliness, level of activity in the session, providing structure to face clients with cognitive, emotional, and behavioral experiences, therapist openness, therapist's ability to adapt to client's preferences, therapist's cultural sensitivity) that contribute in therapy outcome [3, 8]. Researchers using Randomized Clinical Trials (RCTs) studies usually try to control the therapist's variables. However, reanalysis of the most comprehensive evidence-based study on depression (American Psychological Association, Task Force, 1993) identified therapist effectiveness as the main treatment factor; while the treatment models, settings, and even the experience level of therapists were controlled [25]. Also, a meta-analysis of psychotherapy outcome studies [3] has found that clinicians' differences contributed more effect size (0.65) to outcome variance than the treatment models themselves (0.20). Therefore, the therapist's role in therapy outcome is sometimes referred to as a "neglected variable" [28]. Consequently, more research on therapist's competency is critically needed, both for research and training purposes. More specifically, research can explore the core competencies that a systemic therapist needs in working with couple and family systems.

2.3 Relationship factors

Relationship factors are associated with the therapeutic alliance, which involves three components: Bonds, Tasks, and Goals. Bordin [29] defined these components as follows: Bonds refer to the nature of affection in the therapeutic relationship, such as caring, warmth, etc.; Tasks refer to the client and therapist's agreement on therapeutic activities and their credibility; Goals refer to the client and therapist's agreement and cooperation toward what they hope to achieve in therapy. The link between therapeutic alliance and outcome has been well-studied in both psychotherapy and family therapy, though the nature of alliance is more complicated in relational therapy [30, 31].

2.4 Hope factors

Being in therapy, a perceived healing process, itself generates hope in the client; which then contributes to the client's motivation and engagement [15]. However, the presence in therapy itself is not the determinant factor of the client's hope. This is because we assume therapeutic hope is a multifactorial dynamic phenomenon and a product of the interaction between therapist, client, their relationship, and contextual factors, plus the therapeutic rationale. Though the clients enter with different levels of hope and motivation, therapists apply different strategies to increase hope [32, 33]. Sprenkle and Blow [22] suggest that the field needs more research to explore the relationship between hope and change process, and how best to enhance client hope. This is potentially a more challenging theme in relational therapy; since a part of the client's system often becomes hopeless or reluctant while the other part is pushing for change.

2.5 Non-specific mechanisms

Though specific theories use different theoretical concepts and terminology and apply their own specific techniques, all those techniques can be defined in three general categories: Behavioral regulation, Cognitive mastery, and Affective experiencing [20]. That is, two different theory-specific techniques (e.g., family sculpting, empty chair) could activate the same emotional processing/regulation in the client system. Prochaska and Norcross [21] refer to such events as change processes that function between theory level and technique level; which are heuristic strategies used by experienced therapists.

2.6 Common MFT/systemic factors

Family therapists generally identify the field of MFT as a distinct profession because of the systemic epistemology that shifts the focus from the individual to relationship patterns. That is, we live in relational systems in which problems develop and solutions can be created [34]. Accordingly, interviewing a youth without the family makes it more difficult to understand and change his/her problem, and identifying one family member as the entire problem is both wrong from a relational lens and also less helpful [35]. So, the systemic epistemology guides problem definition, treatment rationale, and therapy goals in a manner that is different from those typically associated with individual therapy. All MFT therapies, to varying extents, share these common mechanisms: (1) relational conceptualization of problems, (2) disrupting dysfunctional relational patterns, (3) expanding the direct therapeutic system, and (4) expanding the therapeutic alliance [22].

3. Debate on common factors and model specificity

Advocates of the model specificity have mentioned a few critiques of the common factors model, including: (a) the support for a common factors model mostly comes from meta-analyses that indicated the equivalency of outcomes across treatment models, so it might not scrutinize some potential differentiating variables between models; (b) the common factors need better operational definitions to be researched and understood; (c) there is lack of evidence to show a specific link between the function of particular common factors and therapy outcome; (d) there is a lack of research that compares therapeutic impact of common factors versus model-specific factors; and (e) finally the CFs model is lacking a temporal and conceptual framework to guide therapists over the course of therapy [9, 10].

We believe these critiques are reasonable and should be addressed by multiple research methods to improve the CFs model as an integrative or metatheoretical approach. The results of meta-analyses on outcome equivalency can be interpreted in at least three ways: first, different models may generate the same efficacy but through different mechanisms of change; second, there might be significant differences between therapies' outcome, but we have not used the right research questions/measures/methods to find them; and third, the common change mechanisms can explain the equivalency of outcomes and possible minimal differences [11].

Since the focus of model specificity research is on efficacy and therapy outcome, the advocates of RCTs/ESTs "incorrectly presumed that therapy was consistently applied across therapists and within each case" ([11], p. 3). That is, most RCTs neglected the therapist and client's factors and their phenomenological experiences, which is a significant source of therapeutic variance [7, 15]. As Kazdin [36] mentioned, "many researchers lament that the manuals, including their own, are incomplete and do not reflect the complexity of treatment and scope of the exchanges between therapist and patient" (p. 293).

Meta-analysis research also cannot adequately explain the therapy process, since its results are built on the RCTs data with little attention to the specific therapeutic mechanisms at work. Likewise, the advocates of model specificity camp believe the current CFs approach overlooks the convolution of therapeutic change and the multilevel reality of practice. More specifically, Sexton et al., [10] concluded that "Two reasons lead us to this conclusion. First, common factors are not conceptually clear, operationally defined, or contextualized within a clinical process enough to make them either researchable or understandable. Second, as currently described, common factors are independent factors that are decontextualized from the complex process of therapy" (p. 137).

Neither manualized ESTs nor huge meta-analysis studies can unfold the mechanisms of change in therapy [11, 23]. The core phenomenon in clinical/MFT theories is to explain the process (when and how) of change, and a key reason for the development of integrative models is to maximize the therapeutic change by making use of multiple therapeutic skills. Similarly, the common factors model can play an integrative role in training, practice, and research. It would certainly help, though, if there were clearer definitions of the factors and their interactions; the context and mechanisms through which the factors are activated; and the temporal order they should be used to achieve both proximal and distal outcomes [5, 11]. Such process-progress research can help to capture the therapist and client's phenomenological experiences, which can shed light on the change mechanisms at different stages of therapy [11, 37]. Any research to this end, can contribute to the development of more effective integrative and clinically relevant theories, and overcome a research-practice gap in the MFT field [5, 8, 11]. Process-progress research can be conducted in different forms and based on a variety of measures. For this chapter, we focus primarily on an exploratory qualitative study that examines the therapist's phenomenological experience of using common factors at three stages of therapy. In the next section, we briefly discuss the research procedures and the findings that suggest a chronological map of using CFs.

4. Research design

Qualitative research is appropriate when theory about a phenomenon is lacking or needs improvement [38]. We used a qualitative research design to address our research goal to improve the theorization of the common factors approach. We considered our project as process research or discovery-oriented research; which is concerned with what is happening in the course of therapy [37]. One assumption of such a research method is that the therapist and client behaviors occur differently at various stages of therapy. That is, even the same act/intervention (e.g., alliance, therapist competence) can be used in different contexts and for different purposes. Based on literature [22, 39, 40] we considered three stages of therapy (initial, intermediate, termination), with the assumption that each stage requires a particular set of CFs, specific interaction between the factors, and different phase-based functions/purposes. Since we aimed to get an in-depth understanding of the phenomenon, we used open-ended questions with a focus on participants' phenomenological experience. We used validation strategies such as having other researchers review our procedures, and eliciting feedback from our participants through member checks [38].

4.1 Sampling and participants

A purposeful/theoretical sampling method was used to recruit an expert panel. The goal of theoretical sampling is to find participants who are the most knowledgeable people in the field of study [38]. Our panel consisted of six experts who were willing to provide in-depth and interactional discussion on a Wiki site designed for this purpose. (As is typical of studies of expert opinion, such as Delphi studies, the backgrounds of the participants are more important than the number of participants.). The inclusion criteria for the expert panel included: Ph.D. degree in a mental health field, publication (peer-reviewed articles, book, dissertation) in common factors/integrative therapy, and more than 10 years of teaching and training experience. Our participants' fields of study included clinical psychology, marriage, and family therapy, and counseling. As for clinical orientation, the participants identified themselves as eclectic CBT, integrative psychodynamic, and integrative family systems therapy.

4.2 Data collection

A Wiki page including instruction and three open-ended questions was created. The Wiki allows participants to discuss their own experiences and interactively comment on others. The participants were not told the identity of the other participants to keep the influence of particularly well-known participants to a minimum. The data was considered the results of the participant's opinions and the results of their shared Wiki conversations [41]. The Wiki webpage began with an explanation that included: the research goal and current research gap in common factors; a brief definition of common factors to make sure all participants had similar definitions of common factors; and three open-ended questions related to a successful (70% improvement) relational (couple/family) therapy case that they previously worked with. The questions posed were:

1. How and what common factors did you use to bring about change in the initial stage of therapy?

2. How and what common factors did you use to bring about change in the intermediate stage of therapy?

3. How and what common factors did you use to bring about change in the termination stage of therapy?

The Wiki space was available for 2 weeks, which allowed the participants to come back and complete/edit their work or comment on others' posts. We assigned separate questions for each stage of therapy to collect information related to differential common factors they may have used at different therapy stages.

4.3 Data analysis

Thematic analysis (TA) was used to identify those patterns that were relevant to the specific research question [42]. That is, when and how do expert therapists use common factors in the course of therapy to reach their desired therapeutic outcomes? We conducted thematic analysis both inductively (bottom-up approach) and deductively (top-down approach). The inductive approach created opportunity for development of new themes of common factors (therapy principles) as well as provided explanation that how and when therapist uses particular common factors at specific points of time in therapy (therapeutic procedures). On the other hand, we employed a deductive analysis, as well, because we had predetermined assumptions and definitions of CFs components [22]. In order to increase the rigor of our data, we employed multiple levels of data analysis, from the narrow codes to more abstract dimensions and interpretations. We used Braun & Clarke's [42] framework of thematic analysis, including: (1) Familiarizing yourself with the data, (2) Generating initial codes, (3) Searching for themes, (4) Reviewing potential themes, (5) Defining and naming themes, (6) Producing the report.

5. Research findings

Using thematic analysis, several codes emerged, and specific themes were developed for the initial, intermediate, and termination stages of therapy, including five themes for the initial stage, five themes for the intermediate stage, and four themes for the termination stage (see **Table 1**). The final themes and their definitions for each stage are discussed here:

5.1 Initial stage

5.1.1 Time planning

Though this theme emerged initially in the first stage of therapy, it continued over the intermediate and termination stage too. This theme refers to the therapists' general

Stage	Mechanisms of change	Goal
1	Time planning Hope and motivation are primary goals Family Alliance in early stage Reframing as a general cognitive-systemic mechanism Hope and motivation achieved through different paths	Hope and motivation
2	Engagement in therapeutic tasks Expanding the direct therapeutic system Facing new experiences Trend of progress and relapse Feedback loop Split Family Alliance	Engagement in new functional patterns
3	Attribution of success Inoculation of future relapse Extended therapeutic alliance Maintain achieved goals through different paths	Maintaining the goal

Table 1.
A chronological map of common factors.

strategy in prioritizing particular common factors at each moment throughout the course of therapy. The experts believed that such planning worked as a heuristic strategy that helps them map the sequence of actions in the course of therapy. That is, the expert panel explained they would not jump into task/homework assignments before they built a strong alliance with each client and facilitated hope, motivation, problem rationale, and treatment rationale. For example, during the early sessions, the therapist initially works on therapeutic hope and persuasiveness. For example, one expert stated: *"I think common factors are MOST applicable early in therapy,"* specifically this expert would focus on supporting the client's decision to come to therapy and explaining how therapy might be helpful if the client system *"came reluctantly to treatment because he was embarrassed that he needed help. His expectations were low and he had misgivings about whether psychological interventions could help."*

5.1.2 Hope and motivation are primary goals

This theme indicates that the experts intentionally prioritize the client's hope and motivation in early sessions of therapy, rather than just listening to the client's problem narrative. Though, the expert panel identified with different theoretical backgrounds, all emphasized the development of hope and motivation as their proximal goal in early stage (*"I gained their trust, engendered hope,..."*). Previous research also indicates that both the common factors approach and the model specific treatments approach emphasize the important role of hope and motivation in the early stage of therapy [23, 33]. For example, Functional Family Therapy (FFT) [43] specifically focuses on hope in the first phase of FFT (labeled induction-motivation). That is, the therapist actively works to get the client to believe that the problem can change and that the therapist and therapy would promote the change (*"taking a system from 'demoralized' to 'remoralized' taps into a powerful therapist and client common factors."*).

5.1.3 Systemic alliance in early stage

This theme refers to specific points: First, building an alliance with all family members is a unique challenge in relational therapies (*"I believe the difficulty in working with a system initially, is that different members of system come in with different goals*"). Second, such alliance in early sessions is accomplished through specific mechanisms: (a) an affective bonds with all members by empathy and validation of their positions (*"we gained buy-in and a strong relationship with all members of this family through validating their positions, using their points of view, and aligning with their goals"..."and bonds with all involved (empathy, validation and support)"*); (b) a goal agreement ("*Establishing an alliance early on, especially on the goals dimensions, is a power common factor in early stage therapy*"). Based on our data, we assume the third component (tasks agreement) of alliance usually occurs in the intermediate stage of therapy.

5.1.4 Reframing as a general cognitive-systemic mechanism

This theme, in relational therapies, refers to a general cognitive-systemic procedure that alters the meaning of the client's perceived problem and its relational context. The therapist challenges the definition of the client's presenting problem and creates a new contextual lens; in which the blaming of self and others faded away and so the possibility of transition from stuck position seems doable (*"He had an affair to which she responded in part by starting to drink again after many years of sobriety" or "I offered a clear rationale for each party of the system"*). Therefore, it implies that change is doable and so hope is engendered.

Our data indicate the relational conceptualization of the problem (systemic reframing) not only generates a new systemic lens but also unites the members toward the benefit of the whole system, so contributes both in hope and the within-family alliance [35, 44–46]. Systemic reframing function across all MFT models. For example, Bowen challenges the most "subjective face" of the problem. Haley and the Mental Research Institute (MRI) group challenge "the more of the same," and White challenges the "social dominant systems." Despite the widespread use of reframing in therapy, there is a lack of empirical evidence to explain the impact of this mechanism on family interaction and therapy outcome [33]. Alexander et al. [47] showed lower defensive behaviors following reframe intervention than other types of therapist's interventions (reflection, restructuring statements).

5.1.5 Hope and motivation achieved through different paths

This theme refers to the fact that the hope and motivation as the primary goal of the early stage can be developed via multiple pathways; which are due to a variety of factors (the therapist and client's characteristics, clinical settings, clinical problem, session formats, etc.). Some of the experts achieved the goal through relationship factors and the therapist's presence (e. g., "*I tried hard to maintain a non-reactive presence and validate each of their positions in order to establish safety and increase hope"..."this formed a strong relationship, ..., and engendered hope" or "I also want to emphasize that the most important common factors are reflected more in who the therapist 'is' rather than what the therapist 'does'.*"), which is consistent with some theories (Attachment, Bowenian, Experiential, Emotion-focused). That is, people will be hopeful and explorative when they find themselves in a safe and secure relationship [37]. Other expert used his own expertise/competency (therapist factors) to build trust and, in turn, hope in the client system (*"... to let them know that even though they are freaking out and do not see a way out of it all, it is something that I have seen often, understand, and know how to handle"*), this could be consistent with the Structural-Strategic model [44, 45].

The other mechanisms were problem explanation, goal setting, and treatment rationale that fitted with client's worldview to develop hope and motivation (*e.g., "offered a clear rationale for each party of the system" or "It was also critical that I honored each party's position on the nature of the problem, their values, language, and their goals"*). Also, some of the experts used "breaking dysfunctional patterns" which contributed to hope and motivation through reduction of negativity and blaming in the client's system [33, 45]. The following excerpts illustrate that CFs are not just a list of static factors, but they are prioritized and interactively used to create a context of change (*"I think of common factors as dynamic processes within the larger context of change," or, "Early in treatment as we developed a relationship of trust and warmth and as he learned about treatment, he begins to have hope that he might benefit from treatment. As you can see from this, some therapist, relationship, and hope components were evident. I was using a CBT approach to treatment"*). So, we assume that these hope-generating mechanisms function beyond a specific theory or model, but within the therapeutic participants.

5.2 Intermediate stage

5.2.1 Engagement in therapeutic tasks

This theme refers to the process in which the therapist works with the client system on the assumption that change requires action and responsibility. This process is based on previously activated client's factors (such as hope and motivation, etc.), therapist's factors (support, expertise, etc.), relationship factors (bonds, trust, etc.), and the problem explanation and treatment rationale (*"During the middle phase of treatment, I maintained my treatment rationale (chosen to fit with these clients and the way they viewed their problems)"*). Our participants' experiences indicate some clients easily engage in therapeutic tasks while others are reluctant; which demands the therapist to actively work on this process to get the client system engaged (*"The case I'm thinking about was unique.....they were all seen as resistant or reactive to treatment"..."I gained their trust, engendered hope, and offered a clear rationale for each party of the system"*). Our findings suggest that this mechanism is used by all models. However, the client characteristics and the type of problem determine to what extent a therapist should work on this mechanism (*"I also adapted to their personalities by pushing and challenging them pretty directly throughout this stage – an approach they liked"*). For example, the therapy dropout rates for youth with behavioral and drug problems are estimated from 50–75% [48], which can explain why FFT specifically emphasizes on engagement and motivation of youth and families in early stage of therapy [47].

5.2.2 Expanding the direct therapeutic system

This theme refers to the therapist intention to expand the therapeutic contact to other family members or systems who can facilitate therapeutic change. (*"Mom brought boyfriend into the relationship and they both set clear limits and expectations {for the son}"*). This is another unique systemic CFs that function across MFT therapies, specifically integrative models. For example, multisystemic family therapy (MSFT) expands therapeutic interventions to the wider school and interagency network [49]. The degree of such expansion is based on the relational conceptualization of the problem at stage one as well as the ongoing feedback from the client system to therapy interventions.

5.2.3 Facing new experiences (emotional, cognitive, behavioral)

This theme refers to any new cognitive, behavioral, and emotional experience that helps the client to achieve therapeutic goals. They are new functional patterns that are challenging pathways to achieve therapeutic goals. Some experts used cognitive strategies (*"his insights were also related to the CBT intervention"*) versus others that used emotional strategies (*"processed a lot ala EFT"*), and others used behavioral strategies (*"I develop task assignments aimed at interrupting patterns"..."son began doing his homework and was rewarded by going to work in doing some construction jobs with [the mom's]boyfriend"*). The critical point is the overlap between these apparently content-distinct interventions which all finally result in the same functional pattern (process) in the client system. That is, from an experiential lens there is a concurrent experience of emotional, behavioral, and cognitive aspects in real life. For example, the "blamer softening" technique in EFT is considered primarily an emotional processing intervention but in fact it is associated with promotion in both intrapersonal awareness and interpersonal restructuring of interactions [37]. That is, an emotional schema of self and others changes which, in turn, triggers new behaviors from the partner. However, we assume the therapist's style and client's characteristics and feedback could guide which type of these three mechanisms would be more desirable and applicable. (*"I was calm (that's my overall style/personality anyway,"* or *"My position with her son was to commiserate with his distress over Dad and to empathize with him over how his mother was treating him like a child"*). Even within an evidence-based treatment like Emotion-Focused Therapy (EFT), the therapist's emotional presence (e.g., manner of emotional responsiveness and softened vocal quality) predicts heightened levels of client emotional experience in successful "Blamer Softening," which is a unique indicator of successful therapy [50]. As Lebow [5] noted "therapists vary enormously," so the same cognitive technique, for example, can function unevenly in the change process due to such an enormous variety.

In addition, these new experiences can be done either in the session (*"allowing clients to explore safely their relational problems with the therapist in the 'here and now' context of the therapeutic relationship"*), or out-of-therapy session (*"Son was allowed more freedom and complied by returning home early and pitching in with home chores."*). This distinction between in-session and out-of-session tasks itself is an important research topic in the MFT field.

5.2.4 Trend of progress and relapse

This theme refers to a natural trend of progress and relapse in an intermediate stage of therapy. The experts described it as a process in which the client system normally experiences ups and downs to achieve a new functional pattern, though progressively toward more competence (*"There was a lot of progress, followed by relapse, then progress, then relapse, etc.," or, "'I believe that a successful' 'tear and repair' in the intermediate stage of therapy will strengthen the overall therapeutic alliance by allowing clients to explore safely their relational problems"*). Expert therapists anticipated such a trend, so they inform and inoculate their clients in advance regarding of the trend (*"I have learned to offer inoculations..... to help with this", "you may notice early improvement followed by a backslide"*). By doing precedent inoculation, the therapist prevents hopelessness and alliance rupture as well as inspires more client's persistence and engagement.

Also, it seems the conceptualization of this trend goes beyond individual therapy and contains a wider contextual lens. Our findings indicate a reaction by the client's family of origins and their work following therapeutic change during the intermediate stage (*"there were extratherapeutic factors happened in each of their families as well as their work lives that essentially forced them to either turn towards or away from each other. Therapy helped guide that change"*).

Another sub-theme related to the "trend of progress and relapse" was "ongoing mutual feedback"; which helped the experts to continuously adjust the relationship, their conceptualization, and methods due to improvisational nature of the process (*"I also adapted to their personalities by pushing and challenging them pretty directly throughout this stage - an approach they liked,"* or, *"the concept of giving and eliciting client feedback, is especially essential in later phases,"* or, *"I try to balance being real and authentic about my hopes for them while at the same time creating space for them to chart the course they feel is best"*). Recently, the mutual feedback has received more attention as a critical change mechanism in therapy [5, 11].

5.2.5 Split systemic alliance

This theme refers to a common phenomenon in the intermediate stage of relational therapy in which a part of the client system experiences weaker alliance to the therapist than another part of the system [31]. It causes resistance to engage in therapeutic tasks while the therapist is aiming to unite them toward their therapy goal (*"A split alliance may quickly degenerate into an alliance rupture,"...., "I continued to be open to flex as needed if their alliance was faltering in any ways"*).

To repair a split systemic alliance, the experts approached the client subsystems in one unite as a couple or family system (*"I also relied on the depth of our connection-they knew that I cared about them and that their marriage mattered to me"* or *"she said that she knew that I really wanted them to succeed as a couple, which kept her going"*). They used a few systemic change mechanisms, including relational conceptualization of the problem which takes away the blame from all members; presenting relational patterns as therapeutic target; disrupting conflicted family interactions to reduce negativity [7, 33]; prioritizing the wellbeing of the whole system than any individual member of the system; and presenting emotional neutrality to all members [7, 35].

5.3 Termination stage

5.3.1 Attribution of success

This theme refers to a process that helps the client system to own the therapeutic changes that have been made. That is, the client system internalizes them as a result of their efforts and skills (*"I commended them for all they had done and gave them a chance to explain how they did it thus having them own the change by attributing it to themselves"*). This mechanism is consistent with the self-efficacy concept [51] that is negatively correlated with relapse [52] (*"Here, I want to make sure that I highlight what the client has done to bring about change. I will often make a list and send it home with the client"*).

5.3.2 Inoculation of future relapse

This theme refers to a process in which the therapist educates the client system about the possible relapse after termination, and the strategies can be used to handle a possible relapse (*"Upon successful termination, we commended all and inoculated them against inevitable backsliding and future hurdles"*). Our findings show that the experts used a feedback loop with the client system to help them gain insight about the change process, which itself is a pathway for clients to be able to handle possible future hurdles (*"While important in all stages of therapy, the concept of giving and eliciting client feedback is especially essential in later phases as termination approaches"*).

5.3.3 Extended therapeutic alliance

This theme refers to the availability of the therapist after termination in case the client system needed help or support (*"I extend the relationship by reframing termination as variable scheduling- the client calls me for an appointment if a need comes up"*). By doing this, the therapist intentionally expands the therapeutic alliance beyond the therapy course; which generates security and hope that can contribute to better maintenance of achieved goals.

5.3.4 Maintain achieved goals

This theme refers to the mechanism that helps the client to sustain new functional patterns that they have developed in the course of therapy. That is, the client system earns a capacity to continue the therapy outcomes without depending on the therapist (*"At termination I am working clients on sustaining changes that they have made"*). To this end, the experts utilized several mechanisms: using strengths-based conversations with client; empowering the client to own the changes have been made in therapy; expanding therapeutic alliance available after termination; educating client regarding of future relapse (*"A lot of strengths-based conversation and reflection on the progress they'd made, as well as inoculation against future relapse as has been mentioned by others…." "I also, prepare the client for relapse and develop plans for how to manage a relapse",.., "specific interventions ongoing to help create a situation where changes could be maintained"*).

6. Discussion

Despite disagreements between advocates of the model-specificity approach and CFs approach on outcome equivalency, they agree that the process and progress research can shed light on the mechanisms of change; which can bridge the two approaches and contribute to the field's integration [4, 5, 8]. To this end, we presented a primarily chronological map of common factors at three stages of relational therapy, which is supported by the findings of our qualitative process research and existing MFT literature.

Our findings show that the experts, regardless of their theoretical lens, focused on generating hope and motivation as the primary goal of the initial stage, though they achieved it through different combinations of these CFs (using therapist presence and safe relationship, family alliance, therapist expertise/competency, relational conceptualization of problem, interrupting dysfunctional pattern, and goal agreement). It is consistent with the phased-based goals and challenges in most evidence-based treatments. For example, Functional Family Therapy [43] labels the first stage as "Induction-Motivation," or Structural Therapy [45] labels it as "Joining and Accommodation," though they may use different combinations of the above-mentioned change mechanisms/CFs to achieve the same proximal goal.

The priority goal in the intermediate stage was the engagement in therapeutic tasks, which calls for the client system's responsibility and action toward therapy goals. To this end, the experts utilized the therapist's presence, relationship factors, and the client's hope as a context. However, the main mechanisms were: the relational conceptualization of the problem, systemic goal agreement, and treatment rationale. By doing so, they enhance the credibility of therapy which itself is a mechanism of therapeutic change [13, 53]. As opposed to blaming clients for being uninterested or unmotivated, the experts contextualize the problem explanation and treatment rationale within the client's system and culture to enhance their engagement in therapy [54, 55].

Another important finding was a "trend of progress and relapse" in the second phase of therapy, which was considered to be a natural phenomenon and a systemic reaction to the client's initial change. [47]. We propose the trend of progress and relapse as another unique systemic CFs that should be researched within a systemic perspective. That is, a change in one part/member of the system followed with changes in other parts as well as with support or reaction from neighboring systems [34, 45]. Systemic terminology (such as "symptom exchange," "change back," "social dominant narratives," "ecological model," etc.) can explain the trend of progress and relapse within a relational-contextual lens, which provides more therapeutic options and resources [56, 57]. We believe this common factor represents a unique systemic theme that could contribute to the understanding of change in relational therapy.

As a result of the therapist's effort to get the client system engaged in a task (functional pattern), the client system may react by "split systemic alliance" in which a part of the system experiences weaker alliance and so lower cooperation and engagement in the therapeutic task. Previous research [22, 48] indicates that the nature of alliance in family therapy is different than in individual therapy, due to the complex multiple relationships and competitive demands between the participants [35, 44]. We assume a systemic task asks for redefinition of relationships, power, and positions within the client system, which requires degrees of flexibility and responsibility by the members [47]. Also, it is consistent with the basic systemic assumption of triangulation. This is when a dyad that is not ready to take responsibility in a challenging situation drags the third person into their argument. This third person is often asked to "take sides" [35, 45]. Considering the critical role of systemic alliance in relational therapy outcome and dropout, it is important to explore what mechanisms are used by clinicians across treatment models to handle this challenge and which ones are more effective.

The main goal in the termination stage was to enable the client system to "maintain the achieved goals." The experts applied a few mechanisms to accomplish this goal: first, they used "attribution of success" in which the therapist uses a feedback loop and strengths-based conversation by which the client system explains how they made therapeutic changes. We assume this is consistent mostly with narrative and solution-focused questioning. Telling and re-telling the change a story of success enhances "self-efficacy" and "resiliency" in the client system [52, 58]. Second, they used "inoculation of future relapse" to educate the client system on useful strategies for handling any possible relapses following termination, which is mostly consistent with cognitive theory; third, they "expanded therapeutic alliance" and therapist availability for after termination in case the client system needed help, which generates hope, safety, and resiliency. This mechanism is most closely associated with attachment theory. We assume that integrative therapists apply a combination of these mechanisms that go beyond a specific theoretical model [5, 21].
Previous research [8] indicates that the therapy structure/plan itself contributes to therapy outcome. However, it is specifically important to explore when (if at all) and how clinicians address the termination process with their clients in daily practice. Moreover, what is its impact on therapy length and outcome? We assume this is an important component in the development of a temporal protocol for the use of common factors.

Consistent with other phased-based therapy proposals (e.g., [39, 40]), our findings indicate that common factors function within a phased-based framework. That is, the CFs are used as change mechanisms/strategies with specific proximal process goals at each stage of therapy, not as a list of distinct factors. This primarily temporal protocol of CFs can be used by trainers and trainees as a guide to map the sequence of actions in the course of therapy. Though, there are differences at the theoretical level (e.g., assumption of pathology, importance of relationships versus meaning, etc.) between traditional and post-modern MFT models, both emphasize the same phase-based goals and challenges; which are addressed through almost the same change mechanisms. For example, let aside that it is inconsistent with its collaborative philosophy, Solution-Focused Therapy (SFT) concerns with the clients' motivation level, and labeled them as visitors, complainants, and customers [59]. To solve such a cognitive dissonance at theoretical level, the SFT theorists intended that "the labels were not included; and the descriptions were more nuanced in later years," however, it did not change their actual practice in which they are applying almost the same strategies "normalizations, reframes, new information; and acknowledgment of clients' feelings" to improve the client's motivation level ([32], p. 69, 70). We believe that the field needs to redirect the focus of research and training on these phased-based change mechanisms, which can lead to better clinically relevant and theoretically integrative models [4, 5, 8]. As Kazdin [4] notes, "after decades of psychotherapy research, we cannot provide an evidence-based explanation for how or why even our most well-studied interventions produce change, that is, the mechanism(s) through which treatments operate" (p 1).

Also, our findings indicate that each change mechanism may have a different function at different points of time in therapy process [37]. For example, a relational definition of the problem and/or the therapist's expertise initially are utilized to build hope and motivation, while the same mechanisms are utilized to repair split systemic alliance in the intermediate stage. So, we assume a cyclical/recurring pattern of presence for these change mechanisms, not necessarily a linear one. For example, research [23] indicates that the client's engagement is the single best predictor of outcome. However, the therapeutic relationship may be the most important mediating factor between engagement and outcome.

Based on systemic epistemology that is the core theoretical belief in all MFT models, our findings support the notion that CFs function differently in systemic/relational therapy than individual therapy. As Bateson [34] mentioned "When you separate mind from the structure in which it is immanent, such as human relationships... you embark on a fundamental error," (p. 493). It seems, the pioneers (Bowen, Haley, Whitaker, Fisch, etc.) focused much more on shared underlying family/systemic processes and the relevant systemic change mechanisms than the specific models. This may have contributed in the field to be naturally short-term and integrative, specifically in actual practice [5]. Research supports the notion that CFs should be understood based on systemic concepts and interactional processes when it comes to relational therapies [7, 8, 10]. For example, Functional Family Therapy researchers found that high individual alliance by the adolescent is a predictor of dropout if there is unbalance in adolescent and parents' alliances with therapist [48]. On the other hand, postmodern theories also gradually admitted the power and complexity of dysfunctional patterns in some systems. Lipchik [32], as one of the pioneers of SFT, mentioned that the SFT team gradually modified their theoretical belief that the solution-focused process works, regardless of the type of problem or situation, and so recognized the complexities of some problems and the surrounding systems.

Therefore, it is reasonable to assume that all effective MFT models (including traditional, postmodern, or integrative) deal with the same underlying systemic/interactional processes in actual practice, regardless of their level of theoretical congruency and technical terminology. That is, the clinical research should focus on those change mechanisms (e.g., inoculation, systemic alliance, relational conceptualization, etc.) that can alter such systemic processes (e.g., split systemic alliance, lack of boundaries, etc.) which are common, in some degree, within all clinical problems. So, we need mechanism-based change theories and research that guide us regarding what mechanism to use, when to use it, and how it should be used during the change process.

To that end, process-progress research [37] can help, since it explains the therapist and the client's actions at each point of the change process. Therefore, we can link in-session improvements on critical factors and treatment outcomes [11]. Accordingly, the "practice-based evidence" that is based on client's feedback can inform us about the client's theory of change [23]. Finally, the convergence of the therapist and the client's theories of change will provide useful evidence-based explanations for why and how therapy works, and through what mechanisms. We believe that the chronology of common factors that we present in this paper represents one important step in this direction.

Author details

Hassan Karimi[1*], Fred Piercy[2] and Jyoti Savla[2]

1 Johns Hopkins University, Baltimore, USA

2 Virginia Tech, Blacksburg, VA, USA

*Address all correspondence to: hassan.karimi@jhu.edu

References

[1] Shadish WR, Baldwin SA. Meta-analysis of MFT interventions. Journal of Marital and Family Therapy. 2003;**29**(4):547-570

[2] Barlow DH, Gorman JM, Shear MK, Woods SW. Cognitive-behavioral therapy, imipramine, or their combination for panic disorder: A randomized controlled trial. JAMA. 2000;**283**(19):2529-2536

[3] Wampold BE. The Basics of Psychotherapy: An Introduction to Theory and Practice. : Washington Dc: American Psychological Association; 2010

[4] Kazdin AE. Mediators and mechanisms of change in psychotherapy research. Annual Review of Clinical Psychology. 2007;**3**:1-27

[5] Lebow J. Integrative approaches to couple and family therapy. In: Sexton TL, Weeks GR, Robbins MS, editors. Handbook of Family Therapy. New York, NY: Brunner Routledge; 2015. pp. 219-242

[6] Eysenck HJ. The effects of psychotherapy. In: Eysenck HJ, editor. Handbook of Abnormal Psychology: An Experimental Approach. New York: Basic Books; 1961. pp. 697-725

[7] Davis SD, Piercy FP. What clients of couple therapy model developers and their former students say about change, part I: Model-dependent common factors across three models. Journal of Marital and Family Therapy. 2007;**33**(3):318-343

[8] Sprenkle DH, Davis SD, Lebow JL. Common Factors in Couple and Family Therapy: The Overlooked Foundation for Effective Practice. New York, NY: The Guilford Press; 2009

[9] Chambless DL, Ollendick TH. Empirically supported psychological interventions: Controversies and evidence. Annual Review of Psychology. 2001;**52**(1):685-716

[10] Sexton TL, Ridley CR, Kleiner AJ. Beyond common factors: Multilevel-process models of therapeutic change in marriage and family therapy. Journal of Marital and Family Therapy. 2004;**30**(2):131-149

[11] Pinsof WM, Wynne LC. Toward progress research: Closing the gap between family therapy practice and research. Journal of Marital and Family Therapy. 2000;**26**(1):1-8

[12] Rosenzweig S. Some implicit common factors in diverse methods of psychotherapy. American Journal of Orthopsychiatry. 1936;**6**(3):412-415

[13] Frank JD. Persuasion and Healing: A Comparative Study of Psychotherapy. Baltimore: Johns Hopkins University Press; 1961

[14] Luborsky L, Singer B, Luborsky L. Comparative studies of psychotherapies: Is it true that everyone has won and all must have prizes? Archives of General Psychiatry. 1975;**32**(8):995-1008

[15] Lambert MJ. Psychotherapy outcome research: Implications for integrative and eclectical therapists. In: Norcross JC, Goldfried MR, editors. Handbook of Psychotherapy Integration. New York: Oxford University Press Basic; 1992. pp. 94-129

[16] Karimi H. The contribution of common factors to therapeutic outcomes from the clinician's perspective: A mixed method study to explore common mechanisms of change [Doctoral dissertation]. Virginia Tech; 2015

[17] Grencavage LM, Norcross JC. Where are the commonalities among

the therapeutic common factors? Professional Psychology: Research and Practice. 1990;**21**(5):372

[18] Goldfried MR, Padawer W. Current status and future directions in psychotherapy. In: Converging Themes in Psychotherapy. New York, NY: Springer Publishing Company; 1982. pp. 3-49

[19] Gurman AS, Kniskern DP. The future of marital and family therapy. Psychotherapy: Theory, Research, Practice, Training. 1992;**29**(1):65

[20] Karasu TB. The specificity versus nonspecificity dilemma: Toward identifying therapeutic change agents. The American Journal of Psychiatry. 1986;**143**(6):687-695

[21] Prochaska JO, Norcross JC. Systems of Psychotherapy: A Transtheoretical Analysis. Belmont, CA: Thompson Brook/Cole; 2007

[22] Sprenkle DH, Blow AJ. Common factors are not islands—They work through models: A response to Sexton, Ridley, and Kleiner. Journal of Marital and Family Therapy. 2004;**30**(2):151-157

[23] Duncan BL, Miller SD, Sparks JA. Interactional and solution-focused brief therapies: Evolving concepts of change. In: Sexton TL, Weeks GR, Robbins MS, editors. Handbook of Family Therapy. New York, NY: Brunner Routledge: 2003. pp. 101-124

[24] Erickson MH. Special techniques of brief hypnotherapy. International Journal of Clinical and Experimental Hypnosis. 1954;**2**(2):109-129

[25] Blatt SJ, Sanislow CA III, Zuroff DC, Pilkonis PA. Characteristics of effective therapists: Further analyses of data from the National Institute of Mental Health treatment of depression collaborative research program. Journal of Consulting and Clinical Psychology. 1996;**64**(6):1276

[26] Tallman K, Bohart AC. The client as a common factor: Clients as self-healers. In: Hubble MA, Duncan BL, Miller SD, editors. The Heart and Soul of Change: What Works in Therapy. Washington, DC: American Psychological Association; 1999. pp. 91-132

[27] Miller SD, Duncan BL, Hubble MA. Escape from babel: Toward a unifying language for psychotherapy practice. Adolescence. 1997;**32**(125):247

[28] Garfield SL. Brief psychotherapy: The role of common and specific factors. Clinical Psychology & Psychotherapy. 1997;**4**(4):217-225

[29] Bordin ES. The generalizability of the psychoanalytic concept of the working alliance. Psychotherapy: Theory, Research & Practice. 1979;**16**(3):252

[30] Martin DJ, Garske JP, Davis MK. Relation of the therapeutic alliance with outcome and other variables: A meta-analytic review. Journal of Consulting and Clinical Psychology. 2000;**68**(3):438

[31] Friedlander ML, Escudero V, Heatherington L, Diamond GM. Alliance in couple and family therapy. Psychotherapy. 2011;**48**(1):25

[32] Lipchik E. The development of my personal solution-focused working model: From 1978 and continuing. International Journal of Solution-Focused Practices. 2014;**2**(2):63-73

[33] Robbins MS, Alexander JF, Turner CW. Disrupting defensive family interactions in family therapy with delinquent adolescents. Journal of Family Psychology. 2000;**14**(4):688

[34] Bateson G. The Logical Categories of Learning and Communication. Steps to an Ecology of Mind. Chicago: University of Chicago Press; 1972. pp. 279-308

[35] Bowen M. Family Therapy in Clinical Practice. Lanhan, MD: Jason Aronson; 1985

[36] Kazdin AE. Treatment research: The investigation and evaluation of psychotherapy. In: Hersen ME, Kazdin AE, Bellack AS, editors. The Clinical Psychology Handbook. Elmsford, NY, US: Pergamon Press; 1991. pp. 293-312

[37] Bradley B, Johnson SM. Task Analysis of Couple and Family Change Events. Research Methods in Family Therapy. New York, NY: Guilford Press; 2005. pp. 254-271

[38] Creswell JW, Hanson WE, Clark Plano VL, Morales A. Qualitative research designs: Selection and implementation. The Counseling Psychologist. 2007;**35**(2):236-264

[39] Prochaska JO, Norcross JC. Stages of change. Psychotherapy: Theory, Research, Practice, Training. 2001;**38**(4):443

[40] Tracey TJ, Ray PB. Stages of successful time-limited counseling: An interactional examination. Journal of Counseling Psychology. 1984;**31**(1):13

[41] Castaños C, Piercy FP. The wiki as a virtual space for qualitative data collection. The Qualitative Report. 2010;**15**(4):948-955

[42] Braun V, Clarke V. Thematic analysis. In: Cooper H, editor. The Handbook of Research Methods in Psychology. Washington, DC: American Psychological Association; 2012

[43] Sexton TL, Alexander JF. Functional family therapy for externalizing disorders in adolescents. In: Handbook of Clinical Family Therapy. Hoboken, NJ: John Wiley & Sons; 2005. pp. 164-191

[44] Haley J. Problem-Solving Therapy. San Francisco, CA: Jossey-Bass; 1987

[45] Minuchin S. Families and Family Therapy. Cambridge, MA: Harvard University Press; 1974

[46] White M. Maps of Narrative Practice. New York, NY: WW Norton & Company; 2007

[47] Alexander JF, Robbins MS, Sexton TL. Family-based interventions with older, at-risk youth: From promise to proof to practice. Journal of Primary Prevention. 2000;**21**(2):185-205

[48] Robbins MS, Turner CW, Alexander JF, Perez GA. Alliance and dropout in family therapy for adolescents with behavior problems: Individual and systemic effects. Journal of Family Psychology. 2003;**17**(4):534

[49] Henggeler SW, Lee T. Multisystemic treatment of serious clinical problems. In: Kazdin AE, Weisz JR (Eds.), Evidence-based psychotherapies for children and adolescents. New York, NY: The Guilford Press; 2003. pp. 301-322

[50] Furrow JL, Edwards SA, Choi Y, Bradley B. Therapist presence in emotionally focused couple therapy blamer softening events: Promoting change through emotional experience. Journal of Marital and Family Therapy. 2012;**38**:39-49

[51] Bandura A. Human agency in social cognitive theory. American Psychologist. 1989;**44**(9):1175

[52] Weinberger J. Common Factors are Not So Common and Specific Factors are Not So Specified: Toward an Inclusive Integration of Psychotherapy Research. 2014;**51**:514-518

[53] Shapiro DA. Comparative credibility of treatment rationales: Three tests of expectancy theory. British Journal of Clinical Psychology. 1981;**20**(2):111-122

[54] Muir JA, Schwartz SJ, Szapocznik J. A program of research with Hispanic

and African American families: Three decades of intervention development and testing influenced by the changing cultural context of Miami. Journal of Marital and Family Therapy. 2004;**30**(3):285-303

[55] Chen R, Piercy FP, Huang WJ, Jaramillo-Sierra AL, Karimi H, Chang WN, et al. A cross-National Study of therapists' perceptions and experiences of premature dropout from therapy. Journal of Family Psychotherapy. 2017;**28**(3):269-284

[56] Fishman HC, Andes F, Knowlton R. Enhancing family therapy: The addition of a community resource specialist. Journal of Marital and Family Therapy. 2001;**27**(1):111-116

[57] Liddle HA. Conceptual and clinical dimensions of a multidimensional, multisystems engagement strategy in family-based adolescent treatment. Psychotherapy: Theory, Research, Practice, Training. 1995;**32**(1):39

[58] Walsh F. Family resilience: A framework for clinical practice. Family Process. 2003;**42**(1):1-8

[59] De Shazer S. Patterns of Brief Family Therapy: An Ecosystemic Approach. New York, NY: The Guilford Press; 1982

Chapter 2

Emotionally Focused Family Therapy: Rebuilding Family Bonds

Katherine Stavrianopoulos

Abstract

Relationships with parents, siblings, and other family members go through transitions as they move along the life cycle. Resilient families realign their relationships to respond to the changing demands and stressors within the family system. Those who are unable, find themselves in repetitive patterns marked by conflict and distress, often resulting in their need to seek treatment. Based on attachment theory, Emotionally Focused Family Therapy (EFFT) is a pragmatic short-term treatment approach designed to alleviate distress in family functioning. This chapter provides an overview of EFFT process, its theoretical underpinnings and the strategies EFT family therapists employ to promote positive outcomes. The presentation of a case study provides a unique lens where the therapist illustrates moment to moment interventions in an attempt to create new and more favorable family interactions, ones that enhance family members' feelings of attachment, empathy, communication and stability.

Keywords: emotionally focused family therapy, family distress, adolescence, attachment, negative interactions

1. Introduction

In the last 20 years, research studies have demonstrated the effectiveness of emotionally focused couple therapy (EFT) in helping couples repair their distressed relationships. The natural extension and broader application of EFT couple's treatment can prove especially valuable and effective when working in a family system [1, 2]. The foundational principles of Emotionally Focused Couple's Therapy is based on attachment and bonding theories that aim to help individuals gain a greater awareness of their emotions, to provide them with strategies to effectively cope, regulate, and transform their emotions[3]. It is a short term, evidence-based approach that allows the therapist to set goals, target key processes, and chart a destination for couples to identify and remove those emotional blocks which derail the promotion of healthy functioning, while providing alternative approaches that serve to increase levels of attentiveness, empathy and feelings attachment and belonging with one another.

According to Johnson, [4] EFFT is similar to emotionally focused therapy for couples, except that with families, the goal is "to modify family relationships in the direction of increased accessibility and responsiveness, thus helping the family create a secure base for children to grow and leave from." Working within a larger family system can be especially daunting as therapists attempt to navigate the vast landscape of family dynamics encompassing multiple, complex interpersonal processes between members, especially the powerful bonds that exist between parent and child, which when weak and broken—are often the root of familiar distress and dysfunction. The core of the human experience of a family lies within its ability to create supportive bonds that sustain it during turbulent and stressful times in its life cycle. The application of EFT to family treatment offers a practical, useful and expedient model from which to effectively bolster stronger and more empathic bonds between parents and their children.

This chapter provides an overview of EFFT process, its theoretical underpinnings and the strategies EFT family therapists employ to promote healthy family functioning. Through a presentation of a case study, beginning therapists are provided a unique lens from which to view the interactions of both family and therapist as they attempt to create new family interactions, marked by increased parental accessibility and responsiveness to children, which ultimately leads to their enhanced sense of attachment, communication, belongingness and security.

2. Theoretical framework

Emotionally Focused Family Therapy (EFFT) is an integration of humanistic [5] and systemic therapeutic approaches [6]. The focus of treatment is on the ongoing construction of a family's present experience and how patterns of interaction are organized and expressed between family members. Another significant aspect of EFFT is its detailed attention to emotions. Identifying emotions is viewed by the therapist as essential in how family members view themselves and others, or an event. Emotions are hard wired in our brain and are meant to inform us about our environment. They also, contain physical impulses, which are designed by nature to be an immediate and adaptive call to action. In EFFT, emotions are categorized as primary and secondary. Primary emotions have been identified by researchers as universal emotions, such as joy, anger, fear, sadness, surprise, and shame. These emotions are frequently outside of people's awareness. Secondary emotions are defined as reactions, and they help people cope with their primary emotions. The word "emotion" comes from the Latin word, *emovare* meaning "to move." Emotions are openly identified, shared and often reframed by the EFFT therapist, as a vehicle to help family members navigate into new and more favorable patterns of interaction, one's that are more empathic and capable of building safe and healthier relationships.

EFFT is grounded in attachment theory and based on the work of psychologist John Bowlby [7]. Bowlby maintains that human beings are biologically and fundamentally driven to pursue relationships that create security and belonging. He contends that the most critical attachment relationship is an infant's sense of protection created by the primary caregiver (typically the mother) through a series of reciprocal interactions which promote bonding and love. As Karen [8] in *Becoming Attached* says about love, "You don't need to be rich or smart or talented or funny; you just have to be there." A parent's emotionally engaged presence makes all the difference between disconnection and security. Throughout the cycle children and adolescents reach out to their primary attachment figures when they are in distress. If they experience parents as non- responsive or unavailable, it is natural for them to feel isolated, frightened and anxious. Feelings of insecurity in children are likely to heighten expressions that call for parental reassurance. Conversely, children may engage in behaviors that disengage and avoid their expressions of distress, particularly in moments of need [9–11]. In either scenario the resulting negative relational experiences foster instability and anxiety in the family system.

In EFFT, one's sense of a secure attachment is linked to positive mental health. Children who are securely attached are best able to turn to their attachment figures for comfort and support [12]. Mikulincer and Shaver [13] capture the distinction between these predictable patterns of attachment behavior as shown in their research when they describe the issues of secure vs. insecure scripts. The secure script is: "If I encounter an obstacle and/or become distressed, I can approach a significant other for help; he or she is likely to be available and supportive; I will experience relief and comfort as a result of proximity to this person; I can then return to other activities [13]." However, when the attachment system remains in an activated state, there are two different insecure coping responses. The avoidant (dismissive) approach "includes rapid self-protective responses to danger without examining one's emotions, consulting other people or seeking to receive help from them [13]." The implicit script is, "If I am in distress, I will carry on with other activities." In contrast, the anxious approach is described as always being on guard for threat, and having difficulty receiving comfort. The implicit script is, "If I am in distress, I will reach for you and reach for you and reach for you, endlessly and to no avail."

Attachment anxiety and avoidance are natural responses to the lack of confidence in the parents' emotional availability. Drawing from attachment theory, the EFFT therapist conceptualizes distress in terms of attachment dilemmas in which ineffective responses to attachment needs fuel miscommunication, creating parenting dysfunctions and exacerbating symptoms associated with individual psychopathology [14]. The therapist must obtain a clear understanding of symptoms that generate distress in the family and furthermore, evaluate the parent(s) availability and their children's confidence in their availability. These observations will provide the therapist with information about the attachment quality in the parent–child relationship. Insecure attachment is evident when the parent's capacity for empathy is blocked, giving precedence to feelings of anxiety and anger, thus viewing the child as difficult, antagonistic or uncooperative. In such instance, parents tend to blame the adolescent or child as solely the identified patient and remain oblivious to the underlying emotions, of fear, or sadness that are at play [15]. The EFFT therapist connects the child/adolescent's symptoms to their perception that the caregiver is unavailable and detached. This perception increases a child's anxiety, anger and defensiveness that contributes to the presenting problem [9, 16]. The goal of the EFFT therapist is to work through a series of interventions that reframe the family problem as one arising out of an attachment crisis, and subsequently works to normalize family difficulties without blaming anyone [17]. Key to the EFFT process is understanding and integrating these core theoretical principals.

3. EFFT process: Steps and stages

The process of EFFT is categorized into three stages and nine treatment steps. In the initial four treatment steps, the therapist carefully focuses on assessing the interactive styles of the family and judiciously works to deescalate any conflicts as they emerge. In the middle phases of treatment (steps five, six, and seven), the therapist and family, work in concert to find new ways to establish more secure familial relationships. In the final two steps of treatment, the therapist highlights and validates new patterns of positive interaction. As importantly, the therapist reinforces family members confidence to handle future conflicts and issues now that they are armed with greater empathy and understanding for one another. The stages and steps of EFFT are outlined and discussed below.

3.1 Stage one: Deescalating family distress

Step 1: Forming an alliance and family assessment.

Step 2: Identifying negative interactional patterns that maintain insecure attachment.

Step 3: Accessing underlying emotions informing interactional positions/relational blocks.

Step 4: Reframing the problem in light of relational blocks and negative interaction patterns.

The primary focus in stage one is for the therapist to identify and track behaviors and secondary emotions that fuel attachment insecurities. The therapist guides the family away from focusing on the content of their presenting conflicts, to developing a more attentive awareness about what underlies their expressed difficulties. The therapist accomplishes this task by tracking familial behaviors driven by intense emotion. As therapists understand, in times of distress, family members commonly deal with their feelings and interpersonal behaviors in unproductive ways. Some may withdraw, argue, submit, explain, or engage in other behaviors designed to minimize and distract from their emotional pain. In this stage, the therapist pays close attention to the interactive behaviors of the family and reframes maladaptive or secondary emotional responses in efforts to bring into awareness their negative cycle of interactions. A negative cycle is defined as a predictable interactional pattern that gets repeated and organizes the family around insecurity, rather than vulnerability. Negative cycles are fatiguing and destructive for family functioning. Tracking the cycle interrupts the behavior and reveals for the first time to the family their true underlying emotions and how their current behaviors serve as protective mechanisms to avoid discomfort and pain. Accessing primary emotions such as fear, hurt, and sadness creates empathy among family members, facilitates responsiveness, and helps the family deescalate [18]. During this phase of treatment, the therapist often returns to utilizing tracking interventions to reemphasize to the family the importance of understanding and dealing with the underlying issues of their discontent in order to enhance family stability and healthy functioning.

3.2 Stage two: Restructuring family interactions

Step 5: Accessing and deepening a child's disowned aspects of self and attachment needs.

Step 6: Fostering acceptance of child's new experience and attachment related needs.

Step 7: Restructuring family interactions focusing on sharing attachment needs and supportive caregiving responses.

In stage two, the focus is on deepening and expanding primary emotions and unmet attachment needs, in order to reshape attachment bonds between family members that are more secure and connected. The change event in stage two involves the therapist accessing the needs embedded in the newly expanded primary emotions that drive the negative family cycle; and helping family members learn to identify and request that previously unexpressed core attachment needs be addressed. The therapist intentionally structures interventions known as enactments that function to restructure attachment bonds between family members [14]. Typically, these requests are for direct care, contact, or comfort and the shift is premised on the parent(s) ability to respond to their children's vulnerability. It is very common in this stage to observe parents having the desire to respond in a more emotionally connected way to their child, but their empathy may be restricted. In such instances, the EFFT therapist will work with the parents to develop their capacity and ability to respond in a way that shifts family relationships toward more secure bonds, replacing negative and harmful cycles of interactions.

3.3. Stage three: Consolidation

Step 8: Exploring new solutions to past problems from more secure positions.
Step 9: Consolidating new positions and strengthening positive patterns.

Finally, in stage three of EFFT, positive cycles of bonding are consolidated and integrated into the life of the family. At the end of this stage, the family is best able to integrate new ways of engaging in discussions and investing in greater security [18]. Discussions are characterized by more openness, responsiveness, and engagement among family members. It is imperative for the family to learn how to repair failed attempts to connect outside of sessions. Before termination, the therapist affirms that the family is now able to handle its issues and conflicts by examining and resolving them in new and more effective ways. The therapist also focuses on amplifying the family's vision to include more mindfulness of positive affect, vulnerable reaching, and connection.

4. Core interventions

There are two primary sets of interventions utilized by EFFT clinicians to help families navigate through the various stages of the treatment process. These core interventions are designed to direct families toward developing relational bonds that enhance their security, communication and strength. The first set are interventions for accessing, expanding and reprocessing of emotional experience. The second set are interventions for restructuring the family interactions.

The EFFT techniques used within these categories are described below, followed by an example of a therapist's response to highlight and reinforce a more concrete understanding of the techniques deployed. For a more detailed explanation the reader is referred to the EFT manual [3].

4.1 Accessing, expanding and reprocessing emotional experience

4.1.1 Empathic reflection

Reflect (name, order, or distill) emotional processing as it occurs. Slows down the process, directs and focuses attention inward, helps the therapist attune to the client experience, thus conveying understanding and helps in creating alliance. Empathic reflections need to be specific and vivid in order to move the client into a deeper awareness of their emotional experiencing.

Therapist: "I think I hear you say that you become so anxious about his future that you find yourself wanting to control, wanting to know what he has in mind because not knowing or not having 'a say' is so overwhelming. Is that it? And then you become very critical with your son. Is that right?"

4.1.2 Validation

Conveys that the client is entitled to their experience. Such statements function to affirm, and legitimize, the client's experience as understandable, given the attachment relationship context. Validating statements start with, "it makes sense that you would feel this way, given (state specific context)".

Therapist: "That makes sense to me, that when you feel that things are about to escalate between you and your mom, you go away, and you avoid any conversation. Is that right?"

4.1.3 Evocative responding

Through the use of questions, evocative language, and metaphors the therapist opens up the client's experience and encourages them to take another step toward it

Therapist: "What's happening right now as you hear him say that?" "What's it like for you when she follows you around the house, pushing for your attention?"

4.1.4 Heightening

This intervention intensifies, clarifies, and deepens an emotion through persistent focus, reflection or enactments. Thus, allowing the client to identify and accept their emotional experience. The therapist's pacing, tone and timing are significant. The acronym RISSSC, implying emotional risk [3], represents how this intervention is done: with repetition, images, speaking simply, softly, slowly, and using client's words. The soft tone heightens vulnerability and sooths the dysregulated brain, so the client can process clearly.

Therapist: " This sounds really important, can we stay here for a bit, I think I hear you say that deep down you really go to a bad place, a place where you get the message that you are nothing but a failure in their eyes. A real disappointment for a son, and that makes you feel so sad, so hurt inside."

4.1.5 Empathic conjecture

Therapist offers an interpretation of client's experience, or a hunch seen through the attachment lens. This facilitates a more intense experiencing from which new meanings may arise and an expanded awareness. It is important to convey tentativeness when offering a conjecture and to check if what is communicated matches the client's experience.

Therapist: "As I listen to you, I hear you saying that you are angry about her lack of concern for you, but I see the tears in your eyes and I wonder if you are also saying that you are hurt by her lack of concern. Does that seem to fit?"

4.2 Restructuring interventions

The following interventions are used in EFFT to address the restructuring task:

4.2.1 Tracking, and reflecting interactions

Reflections that track family members behaviors slow down and clarify the interactional process.

Therapist: "So, when Alex gets frustrated and walks away ignoring what you say, you get angry too and follow him. You need him to listen to you. And, when your mom follows you around wanting your attention it makes you shut down even more."

4.2.2 Reframing

Reframing interactions in the context of the negative cycle, and attachment needs. An attachment reframe functions to access a positive meaning or intention for a seemingly negative response. It shifts the view of the member to a positive portrayal.

Therapist: "You don't experience that the louder she gets, the more desperately she is trying to find you. It sounds as if she is upset with you, but she is doing everything she can to get close to you."

4.2.3 Creating enactments

The therapist requests direct sharing of a clearly distilled message from one family member to another. Enactments, the most powerful intervention in EFFT, their function is to heighten emotional experience and reshape new interactions among family members which lead to positive cycles of accessibility and responsiveness.

Therapist: "Can you tell her, 'I go away because I don't want things to get worse between the two of us.' Can you tell her this?"

5. Case illustration

To help illustrate EFFT treatment in action, a case study of a family recently seen by the author is provided below:

The Aldo Family: Presenting Concern and Relevant History

The family is composed of James and Penny (names and identifying information have been altered), a professional couple in their early 50s, married for 28 years. They have two children; Ellie (23) and Alex (19). The couple has been on and off in couple therapy for a year. The presenting problem described by the parents focused on their son Alex, who had told them at the end of his third semester in college that he wanted to drop out because "this kind of education" was not for him, and he did not see how it would help him get a job. Both parents were very upset and after much discussion, hesitantly agreed to allow him to take a "gap year." It was their understanding that after the year break, Alex was to resume his studies. During that time Alex worked as a waiter, earning spending money while living at home. His work hours provided him with the flexibility to develop an online business that in the long run became a source of income. Alex enjoyed being independent and learning about the world through travel, reading and much You Tube video viewing. A year later, his goal was to be an entrepreneur and not re-enroll in university. Both parents were extremely upset with Alex and had tried to talk "some sense" into him, but to no avail. It was at this point that Penny- the mom requested a family session.

During the first two sessions the therapist met once with the entire family in order to assess they viewed the problem; and once individually with Alex, in order to develop an alliance and get to know him better. Alex, was a slender young man with short blond hair, and green eyes. He appeared younger than his years and was soft spoken as he stated that he was eager to start the process. Alex perceived his mother as critical, with strong opinions about a college education and persistent about him returning to school. This made him angry and he said that he frequently avoided conversations with her because they always ended up on the topic of his future. Mom viewed her son as unreasonable, and disrespectful because he ignored her questions and refused to engage with her. She experienced him as spoiled, entitled and selfish; this made her feel frustrated. James agreed with his wife and said that the tension between Alex and his mother stressed him, but he did not know what to do to resolve the issue.

Right from the start the EFFT therapist aims to understand the ways family members react to each other and tracks their interaction pattern. As family members discuss how they each perceive their concerns, reactive emotional responses are expressed or suppressed, thus allowing the therapist to witness the negative interaction pattern firsthand. The therapist tracks and reflects the behaviors that elicit the negative response and begins to identify the family pattern that is associated with the problem [3, 4]. It was obvious that this family was caught in a reactive pattern of defensiveness, which escalated with increasing anger and frustration. The family's escalation included mom trying to advise Alex and Alex avoiding the conversation.

The more mom insisted in engaging him the more Alex ignored her and she would get so upset that she would turn to her husband for help. James, not knowing what to do would try to calm her by promising he would talk to Alex. However, his approach was not successful either. The more they tried to talk to him or present him with consequences for his actions, the more Alex pulled away. The more he pulled away, the less valued they felt. It appeared to be a hopeless situation.

5.1 EFFT therapeutic interventions

5.1.1 Stage one: Family De-escalation

What follows is an actual dialog from the initial sessions with the family. This excerpt highlights the goal of stage one treatment to track the cycle between Alex and his mom and attempt to deescalate the tensions between family members.

ALEX: Well, yes... she is unbelievable. She asks me questions, a lot of questions about what I am going to do with my life and I do answer her but a few days later she is asking me the same questions!

THERAPIST: all these questions coming your way, regarding your future and you answer them, and then she asks again. Is that right?

ALEX: Yes, it's so frustrating because it's like, does she not remember? What's going on?

THERAPIST: I can understand your frustration- because, you wonder 'isn't what I say important enough to remember' Is that right?

ALEX: yes, that's exactly right.

THERAPIST: When your mom asks the same question, what happens inside you? What do you say to yourself?

ALEX: I hear myself saying, what is the point? I get frustrated.

THERAPIST: Are you feeling frustrated right now?

ALEX: Yes!

THERAPIST: Would you be willing to stay curious with me for a moment about this part that feels frustrated? Do you notice it somewhere in your body? (*staying with emotion in his body slows him down and intensifies the feeling*).

ALEX: I feel tightening in my chest and my shoulders.

THERAPIST: you hear your mom asking another question about your plans, you get frustrated, which you notice as a tightening in your chest and shoulders, is that right?

ALEX: yes.

THERAPIST: And then what does this frustrated part want to do or say to mom?

ALEX: It wants to avoid her.

THERAPIST: How do you do that?

ALEX: By ignoring her and eventually leaving the room.

THERAPIST: What would happen if you did not ignore her and did not leave; if you stayed and talked with her?

ALEX: Nothing good would come out of that. I will only disappoint her again. There is no point.

THERAPIST: So, if talking makes it worse and you worry that you will disappoint her, then it makes sense that you do not want to engage. It sounds like when these fights happen there is nothing more to do but leave. Is that right?

ALEX: That seems to be the best option, right then and there.

THERAPIST: It makes sense to me that you leave the conversation to avoid making things worse between the two of you and, not disappoint your mom. Do you think your mom knows this? Can you tell her that you leave in order to not escalate things between the two of you?

ALEX: (turning to mom) I do not get into it with you and I walk away because I do not want us to fight and I do not want to disappoint you.

MOM: I had no idea.

THERAPIST: Yes (nodding). This is something new you are learning about Alex.

The therapist also works with mom to identify her behaviors, thoughts and feelings as they relate to the negative cycle.

THERAPIST: And when he walks away what happens to you?

MOM: I get fired up and I follow him, and I ask again. I insist that he listens to me and not ignore me.

THERAPIST: Would you be willing to stay curious with me for a moment about this part that gets all fired up? Do you notice it somewhere in your body?

MOM: I feel tense all over.

THERAPIST: you see Alex walk away, you get very angry, which you notice as a tension all over your body, is that right?

MOM: Yes.

THERAPIST: And then what does this angry part do or say to Alex?

ALEX: It gets very focused, very energized, and follows him relentlessly to get his attention.

THERAPIST: What would happen if you did not do that?

ALEX: I would not know what he is up to and I would not be able to help him. I have good advice- I have been where Alex is now, and I can possibly spare him the heartache if he would talk with me. I worry that he will make a mistake, but he does not value my input.

THERAPIST: You want Alex to value your advice. So, you get angry and you insist on engaging in a conversation in the hopes that you can help him see the value in what you say. Is that right?

MOM: That's right.

THERAPIST: What does it feel like when you think that Alex does not value you?

MOM: (deep sigh) It feels sad.

THERAPIST: You want him to value you and your input and when he does not that makes you feel sad. Is that right?

MOM: (in soft voice) yes.

THERAPIST: Do you think Alex knows that? What would it be like to share a little bit of that with him? That underneath your anger you feel sad because you think that he does not value you? Can you tell him that?

5.1.1.1 Treatment focus and progress in stage one

In the above excerpt the therapist looks at the pattern as it unfolds in the room between Alex and his mom. Family de-escalation occurs as Alex and his mom begin to understand their part in the negative interaction pattern and how their attachment-driven behaviors trigger predictable responses in each other. In this case every time mom needed to be assured that Alex was on the right path regarding his future, she asked questions which in turn triggered Alex and made him feel that an argument was imminent and he would disappoint his mother. He then pulled away to avoid the argument, leaving mom to feel sad and not valued and fearful that she was failing as a mother. This triggered mom and she then followed Alex around the house insisting that he engage with her. Alex would get more frustrated and eventually would leave the room thus confirming mom's fear of not being valued. The therapist helps both uncover these deeper emotions and then invites them to do an enactment. In other words, to turn toward each other and engage in a different conversation. Until now, neither was aware how they protected themselves in their relationship nor had they been able to talk about their underlying feelings. The enactment is successful, and both Alex and mom have a new understanding about each other's behavior. He expresses that he values her and wants to be able to talk with her without arguing because it does not feel good to either of them. They both share in the new experience of staying engaged. This awareness shifts the focus from blaming each other to owing their contribution in the negative cycle. In turn, this begins to alter their experience; they feel calmer and more open. A level of safety is created that will allow us to go deeper into vulnerabilities in the next stage.

5.1.2 Stage two: Restructuring family interactions

What follows below is an example of actual dialog used to illustrate the process of restructuring family dynamics:

THERAPIST: A few sessions ago you talked about feeling sad because you see yourself as a disappointment for your parents. Do you remember?

ALEX: Mhmm.

THERAPIST: I guess, I am curious to know, more about this place that you go to... when you feel that... you are a disappointment. Is it okay for us to go to that place?

ALEX: Sure. (pause) It's pretty bad. I try not to think about it. Instead, I just try to focus and work harder.

THERAPIST: It's so bad that you try to not think about it? Right now as we are thinking about it, talking about, notice what happens in your body.

ALEX: I feel flushed and I feel tightness in my throat. It's a bad feeling. That's why I do not like to think about it.

THERAPIST: Sure, it makes sense. And... who sees you in that place? Who knows about that?

ALEX: Nobody knows. Nobody sees how much I try to make them proud of me. Instead I am told that everything I do is wrong. My whole approach is wrong, I am all wrong! (eyes closed).

THERAPIST: That's really painful—it's hard for you.

(Long Pause)

ALEX: Sometimes it feels that I might be running out of time... you know... my dad had problems with his heart last year. (At this point Alex, with his eyes closed and tears running down his cheeks, can hardly speak. After a long pause he continues). I am afraid that I might not have the chance to prove myself and it will be too late. And that maybe I should give up on my ideas and listen to theirs because it will be faster, but then I get conflicted and I think that, it's not right to do something that I do not believe in. And I really believe in this. I do not want to disappoint them but I do not want to disappoint myself either.

THERAPIST: Wow! It feels like you are running against time and you have to choose - your parents or yourself. Neither is a good option; and so you go here and you struggle, and you are confused and scared and alone trying to figure things out.

Alex is sobbing, and his dad reaches over and hugs him. His mom moves over and she too, sits beside him and hugs him.

THERAPIST: Alex, your parents are right beside you. They want to understand. Can you let them in to that place where you are alone and sad?

ALEX: I am scared when I think that something suddenly might happen to dad or to you (mom) like last year- and then you would not have the chance to see what I accomplished and be proud of me. Then you will never know that I am capable and that it's ok to do it my way.

THERAPIST: That is scary, to think that something might happen to either of your parents and trying to prove yourself, trying to get it right and not disappoint while you still have time.

DAD: I am so sorry that you are so hurt. I am, *we* are not disappointed in you and *we* do not want to "fix you" or "change you". We love you no matter what you do and now that I know I will do anything to be there for you. I am sorry that our pushing- our way of trying to help you caused you so much pain. We love you and want to support you, in a way that is best for you.

ALEX: I could leave the house, but I really want to work on our relationship, because it is important that I, have both of your "blessings" as I move on. It is important, that I leave "the nest" as you say, knowing that you are proud of me and you love me, even if I failed. It's like, the baby bird trying to fly out of the nest. The parents have to trust that he can do it- although they may not know for sure. If the baby bird falls, he needs his parents to lovingly encourage him to try again. Sometimes, he flops around for a little bit before the parents rush in to help, and that is ok. The little bird is learning even if he falls, even if he breaks a wing. Keeping the bird in the nest or constantly giving him directions how to fly is constraining—he will not find *his* way. I guess what I am asking is... do you think you can be there as I try to figure things out? I want to find *my* way and can you trust that I will be okay–without flying in to help me or try to change my path?

DAD: "I had no idea that you felt this way; that you have been trying to fly out of the nest. I didn't see all this as your attempt in figuring things out. What I thought I saw, was a little bird taking advantage of the safety provided by our nest and unless we pushed, you were not going to fly. I see now how that hurt you and how it made you feel that we didn't trust you. I love you and want to support you and it's pretty incredible to hear what has been going on for you."

At this point Alex is weeping in his father's arms. Mom joins in the hug and after a small pause, with tears in her eyes says:

MOM: "I am so sorry I hurt you. I get scared and I rush in to help you, to save you, to show you and that makes you feel that I don't believe in you. I want to be there for you. I don't want you to feel this way."

5.1.2.1 Treatment focus and progress in stage two

In the above excerpt, Alex begins to talk about how scary it is to feel that he disappoints his parents and how he wants to make them proud before he loses either of them. His parents remain open hearted and open minded as he engages with them from a vulnerable place. They see his pain, hurt and fear. Dad not only sees from afar this terrible place that his son struggles in but can stand side by side with him there. His presence is felt, and his apology makes a huge difference to Alex. For the first time, Alex feels seen and feels understood at a much deeper level and therefore, this allows Alex to clearly articulate his attachment needs. Mom and dad worked together to respond to Alex. Often parents cannot empathize because they get caught up in their own secondary responses of fear. Staying present with Alex in his vulnerability allowed both parents to experience how Alex's problematic behavior was related to the family's negative cycle of interaction. In a later session, both parents were able to articulate their fear of failure and Alex was able to hear this and understand much of their stress as parents. He then reassured them, "you have been great parents, given me so much. I hope to be able to offer my kids what you have offered me. I love you both and I don't want you to feel that you have failed as parents." Additionally, he expressed regret for his past behavior toward his mother.

Alex began to ask for contact, and this continued in following sessions which helped to bring them closer together.

5.1.3 Stage three: Consolidation

What follows below is an example of actual dialog used to illustrate the process of consolidation:

MOM: Things are good. Alex initiated a conversation earlier this week where he confided in me and asked for my advice. He was telling me about an incident that happened at work and how he handled it. And then asked for my opinion–how I would have handled it.

ALEX: (smiling) "That was nice, and different than times in the past. She did not do anything, other than just listen.

(Turning toward his mom) You did not try to fix or problem solve with me the way you used to with all the questions. You listened to me for a long time and then I remember that I asked you for advice. You said that you agreed with how I handled the matter and you would have done the same. It really felt good to talk to you like an adult without running away or avoiding you. I want to say, thank you for that because I feel less tense and more relaxed.

THERAPIST: That's really great Alex that you felt good to approach your mom and discuss something that was important to you and ask for her input. And it sounds that you both had this conversation in a different way than before. In a way that even feels different in your body.

ALEX: Yes. Growing up and doing things differently than the way your parents expect is hard and can be kind of scary. Knowing that they are open and that my mom is there without judging me feels great.

MOM: I am so glad that we turned a corner. I am always here for you, no matter what and I want to be the mom you want me to be.

5.1.3.1 Treatment focus and progress in stage three

In the above excerpt mom discovers during treatment that she could help her son by her attentive presence. She understands that she did not have to solve Alex's problems or go "undercover" to find out what he was doing and, as a result, this helped her stay more connected with him. The relationship became safer, closer, and more equal. Both were able to confide in and support each other which is the desired outcome for stage three treatment.

6. Conclusions

Treating families in distress is extremely challenging for family therapists. Professionals working with families, especially neophytes, commonly feel uncertain and discouraged as they attempt to navigate the vast landscape of family dynamics encompassing multiple, complex interpersonal processes between members. As a result, family therapists find themselves negotiating or offering solutions to presenting problems, rather than focus on the underlying issues that are at the root cause of the dysfunction. Unfortunately, they soon realize the techniques used are not effective, and before long the family members cycle back where they started from. This makes the therapists feel inefficient and ineffective and therefore may shy away from doing family work.

Having access to a practical, organized and effective model for working with families is pivotal if practitioners are to make meaningful differences in the lives of people they serve. EFFT arose from the realization that the change principles used in EFT could be applied to family relationships thus changing the cycles of interaction [3]. EFFT is a powerful and efficient way to assess and create positive change within the family system. At its core, EFFT views family distress as a result of attachment insecurity where family members fail to get their attachment needs met. Such families do not possess the skills necessary in expressing their attachment needs and protect themselves by becoming defensive, beginning a negative cycle of interaction which prevents healthy family functioning and stability. Accessing underlying attachment-related emotions and the needs associated with these emotions opens the family to address needs in new ways [3]. Corrective emotional experiences create safety that change family relationships and most likely impact future generations. Tapping into parents' unconditional love is powerful; it offers families great hope and holds tremendous promise in revitalizing the field of family therapy.

Author details

Katherine Stavrianopoulos
John Jay College of Criminal Justice, The City University of New York, New York, USA

*Address all correspondence to: stavros@jjay.cuny.edu

References

[1] Bloch L, Guillory PT. The attachment frame is the thing: Emotion-focused family therapy in adolescence. Journal of Couple & Relationship Therapy. 2011;**10**(3):229-245

[2] Stavrianopoulos K, Faller G, Furrow JL. Emotionally focused family therapy: Facilitating change within a family system. Journal of Couple & Relationship Therapy. 2014;**13**(1):25-43

[3] Johnson SM. The Practice of Emotionally Focused Couple Therapy: Creating Connection. 2nd ed. New York (NY): Brunner-Routledge; 2004

[4] Johnson SM. The Practice of Emotionally Focused Marital Therapy: Creating Connection. New York (NY): Brunner/Mazel; 1996

[5] Rogers CR. Client-Centered Therapy. Boston: Houghton-Mifflin; 1951

[6] Minuchin S, Fishman HC. Family Therapy Techniques. Cambridge (MA): Harvard University Press; 1981

[7] Bowlby JA. Secure Base. New York (NY): Basic Books; 1988

[8] Karen R. Becoming Attached: First Relationships and how they Shape our Capacity to Love. New York (NY): Oxford University Press; 1994

[9] Bowlby J. Attachment and Loss: Separation. Vol. 2. New York (NY): Basic Books; 1973

[10] Johnson SM. Emotionally Focused Couple Therapy with Trauma Survivors: Strengthening Attachment Bonds. New York (NY): Guildford Press; 2002

[11] Kobak R. The emotional dynamics of disruption in attachment relationships: Implications for theory, research, and clinical intervention. In: Cassidy J, Shaver P, editors. Handbook of Attachment: Theory, Research, and Clinical Applications. New York: Guildford Press; 1999. pp. 21-43

[12] Shaver PR, Mikulincer M. Attachment-related psychodynamics. Attachment & Human Development. 2002;**4**:133-161

[13] Mikulincer M, Shaver PR. Attachment in Adulthood: Structure, Dynamics, and Change. 2nd ed. New York: Guildford Press; 2016

[14] Johnson SM. Listening to the music: Emotion as a natural part of systems theory. Journal of Systemic Therapies. 1998;**17**:1-17

[15] Kobak R, Mandelbaum T. Caring for the caregiver: An attachment approach to assessment and treatment of child problems. In: Johnson S, Whiffen V, editors. Attachment Process in Couple and Family Therapy. New York: Guildford Press; 2003. pp. 144-164

[16] Miccuci JA. The Adolescent in Family Therapy: Breaking the Cycle of Conflict and Control. New York: Guildford Press; 1998

[17] Palmer G, Efron D. Emotionally focused family therapy: Developing the model. Journal of Systemic Therapies. 2007;**26**:17-24

[18] Johnson SM, Bradley B, Furrow J, et al. Becoming an Emotionally Focused Couple Therapist; the Workbook. New York: Brunner-Routledge; 2005

Chapter 3

Family Therapy: New Intervention Programs and Researches: Systemic Family Approach in Health Care

Hamilton Lima Wagner and Tania Dalallana

Abstract

Talking about family practice is talking about family systemic approach. There are many cues that are so important to understand how the family functions. This is the scope of systemic family approach, where the health is influenced by all the systems a person belongs. In this chapter, we will discuss how a family interacts and the roles of every person in the family—as individuals and as part of the context. And most of it is how this interaction influences the health of every member of the family. Based on the systemic theory, we will run over some tools that will allow to assess the family and discuss how to ease the communication and to help the family to face their difficulties.

Keywords: systemic thinking, complexity, systemic family therapy, intervention tools

1. Introduction

There is a huge evolution on the health care, medicine, nursery, psychology, pharmacy, and many others fields of care, but most of it has been based on traditional science that analyzes details, but it misses the context.

Many authors had emphasized the need to understand how things are happening and why there are differences between individuals. That is where we find out a new paradigm which is emerging from everywhere but specially in the health field. As the evolution of scientific research in the field of health is more focused on the biomedical model, the emergence of a new paradigmatic movement proposes the reading and understanding of the health/disease interface through the multidetermination of the elements that compose it; according to Khun [1], p. 126, "Scientific revolutions begin with a growing feeling, then also restricted to a small division of the scientific community, that the existing paradigm no longer functions properly in the exploration of an aspect of nature whose exploitation previously driven by the dominant paradigm."

The disease is no longer understood only from the biological point of view, and today it has a very complex conceptual expansion, involving physical, psychological, social, cultural, spiritual, and ecological dimensions.

Systemic thinking does not deny the importance of traditional research, but it is realized that it is not enough to answer the differences between individuals and does not answer many questions about why people suffer of something. So it is necessary to open the mind for these paradigms, where things are complex and complexity will allow the recognition of how to understand and help people and their context to face the challenges life is presenting.

 IntechOpen

Since 1975, Bertalanffy [3] had introduced the systemic thinking in health assistance, but it was Morin in the beginning of the 1970s who had started to talk about complexity and its implication on modern science. From these time and forward, many authors had produced research over these fields, and one of them—Ian McWhiney, a family doctor—had pointed that there is a need of a new approach to offer a health assistance that allows a view of the entire system and to recognize that the ill and illness are part of lifestyle, relations, and social conditions.

Simultaneously, the biopsychosocial model had been proposed by Engel in 1977, and the family theory had started to produce its first researches. The new paradigm recognizes that there are no observers that are out of the system, and it means that their own knowledge and life story will have some influence in the results. That is a major change in the research field and shows one of the big challenges to everyone who works on this field.

2. Systemic family thinking

As long as it is accepted that the family is a system, part of the society where it belongs, many issues appear to be of concern—first is that any system desires to keep its functionality. As a living system, they want to discover their own rules to work, the society rules that allow interaction with other families and organizations of this community. But also they have to admit that each member has their own necessities and will develop according to their possibilities.

That system needs to grow and differentiate to survive, and any movement in every part of the system can challenge the role of the system. This concept shows the complexity to work on this field, but it opens the possibility to understand why people suffer and in the meantime can have some illness or even if nothing can be done can develop an ill.

Life is very complex; we deal with changes in our body, during the time and with the relations with our family—creating a huge challenge to adapt each one with these. But few persons are aware with these challenges. Mostly, they say that is a phase or a crisis, and they do not realize that each moment can stress the system and can develop some noise on the relation.

Every system has roles that must be assumed by their members, and as long it is well divided, it will work more easily; but most of the time, this task division is unfair for some of the members, and it can create stress factors. Every member of the system has some expectations about the others members, and generally it is not clear for everyone what is expected. Members of any human group will interact based on their feelings, but also over the expectations of their counterparts, but they used to understand the others by reflecting over themselves.

This is the field where a systemic professional must work. And there is much more: every person has been built based on the roles that they found early in their lives, as long as they saw the childhood of their mothers and fathers and how the adults related to each other—everyone brings these in their personality, and the ability to face this challenge is the key to the family success (**Figure 1**).

The fortress that every person possesses is based on the skills developed during the childhood: ability to feed, to bond to each other, to organize life, to be protected and to protect others, to find their own limits and to define others' limits, and how to drive their own feelings in any direction. Their learnings are essential for a person to relate with the world that surrounds them. But friendship, affection, and sexuality are also developed in this environment [3].

It is clear that knowing about the family development allows the professional to have a better understanding about the difficulties that have been faced

DOI: http://dx.doi.org/10.5772/intechopen.84582

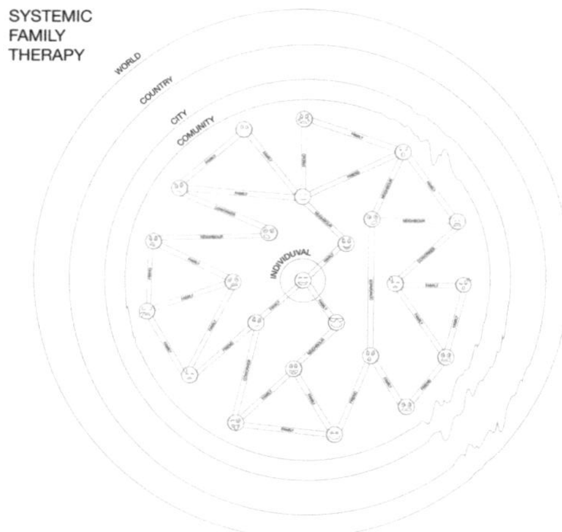

Figure 1.
Schematic functioning of the family system.

by individuals and groups. And the way to describe these situations needs to be understood in order to allow a therapeutic approach and offer some paths to people to have a better life.

3. The steps to working with families

Working with families can be divided into different steps in a different way for better explanation and understanding [6]. The use of these steps depends on the given situation and the needs of each family served. The following phases can be identified schematically: association, evaluation, health education, facilitation, and reference.

3.1 Family connection

Associating with the patient and their family is a fundamental requirement for the construction of the therapeutic process that should be actively pursued. The interaction of the professional with the patient is rich when the former can respect the reality and beliefs of the latter, which is often very difficult. The reality of people's lives is very diverse and demands from the professional a careful observation not to slip into attitudes centered on their own way of seeing life and to believe in solutions based on their core of knowledge. Almost all people receive good advice when they reflect their way of seeing and feeling an item; the attitude of the professional to perceive the situations by their angle of vision can put him in confrontation with the patient and his family, leading to a break in the relationship between them.

Often the professional's lack of practice in working with families leads to the difficulty of understanding why it is necessary to meet with family groups or even to visualize the feelings of each patient. Freire [7], in one of his several texts on pedagogy, approaches in a very clear way the need for the perception of personal experiences in the construction of effective communication. For this communication to take place, it must be based on the lived reality and be of adequate complexity to the person to be reached.

The professional who intends to perform his task of promoting the health of the community where he serves should be able to seek association with patients and their families. In order for this attempt to be achieved, there are some important steps to remember:

1. The moments of contact with the patient and his family are all precious; sometimes a relationship established over time can be broken by disrespecting family beliefs or hierarchies.

2. When it is proposed to contact a patient's family, it is often difficult to see the professional (who is not clear about why a family interview is being conducted) or the patient (who fears losing his status with the professional when the other family members participate).

3. There are pitfalls that this type of intervention can easily expose the professional: family members try to triangulate with the professional, lateralization of communication with one of the family members, the use of language inappropriate for that family group, and disrespect to the group hierarchy and their communication times.

4. The association with the patient and his/her family is the key to making primary health care no longer just a health model, a fad, but actually promoting an improvement in the health and life of the communities served.

The association is initiated when the patient brings to the professional a situation where the family (or the group with which it interacts) interferes directly or indirectly in the process. Often the role of the identified patient is compromised by a clinical or social intercurrence, necessitating adjustments in the family structure, which is a very rich moment to establish a partnership with the group.

3.2 Evaluation

Once the bond with the family has been built, it is important to evaluate it through analysis tools that allow, in a more objective way, to perceive the functioning of the group being studied. These tools seek to explain the power and decision lines of the family, their way of perceiving the health and disease process, their natural resources, and their internal and community support [8]. It is from this analysis that the intervention plan will be proposed, recognizing the belief of the family in the process of becoming ill and negotiating with it an action plan that respects their way of life.

The evaluation of the family group, a clinical task of situation analysis, allows the primary care professional to understand the ways in which the different health conditions arise, such as why alcoholism has a high family incidence or why a patient with hypertension has difficulty controlling their hypertension. Minuchin [9] describes the situation of identical twin sisters with diabetes mellitus who had unequal control of their disease; when analyzing the family relations of these girls, it is found that the one who had a bad control of the disease was the one that triangulated with the parents in their problems of relationship—whenever they fought she made a crisis in their diabetes. It is common to comment in classes on hypertension that if the patients follow the professional's guidelines, they would not have consequences of their disease, but unfortunately the hypertensive patient is very difficult to deal with. This frustrates the results even though the new medications available are highly effective.

The proper evaluation of the role that the person carrying the disease has in his/her family structure (how this illness is perceived by the various components of the group, in what things they believe or like to do) gives the professional an intervention power that increases in the proposed intervention. The use of alcohol in family rituals and their insertion into happy times said by the family lead people to have difficulty understanding it as a health hazard or to glimpse the frequent drinking situation as an initial step toward addiction. Any intervention that proposes to face the problem of alcoholism should consider its symbology for the target group and use the lines of force of this group to obtain an adequate result in the prevention and treatment of the pathology.

Coping with chronic diseases such as hypertension [10] should understand how the patient and his family understand the disease, translating into their language what hypertension is and how the modification of habits can influence the evolution of the process. This type of negotiation is only possible if the process of association and evaluation has occurred satisfactorily, which will allow more consistent and long-lasting results in the follow-up of any patient.

Among the evaluation tools that we can use in primary care, we will list some that are particularly useful, focusing briefly on its use and application. Beginning with the genogram [8, 11], which is an auxiliary graphic instrument in the identification of patterns of repetition of pathologies and behaviors, allowing a quick visualization of the actions to be developed by the study family.

The family life cycle [8, 12, 13] is another powerful tool that identifies situations where the onset of dysfunctions is more frequent. It is in the transition phases where the family is challenged to structure a new pact that stress grows, allowing the emergence of diseases. The life cycle analysis allows the family to assist in understanding the tasks that must be fulfilled in order to cross these transitions.

A third instrument is the social network [14], which allows us to glimpse the support and beliefs of the family. It makes it easier to see who are the key people for the search for support and on what cultural basis we will be interacting with the family. The richness of contacts and community structures allows the search for solutions from the very core, creating the bases for self-care.

Fundamental Interpersonal Relations Orientations (FIRO) [8, 15] is an instrument that analyzes the family from the dimensions of inclusion, control, and intimacy. Inclusion is the starting point—what is to be understood in the levels of group structure, beliefs that provide the behavioral guidelines of the group, and the roles to be played by each member for the harmony of the group. Once included the individual develops some type of control within the group and established the type of control conditions are created for the development of intimacy. FIRO provides conditions to understand the meanings of the different processes that occur in the study group, helping in the planning of the action.

There are a number of other family assessment instruments that can be used in accordance with the training and preparation of the primary care professional, and this chapter does not aim to exhaust the various instruments to exhaustively detail those mentioned. In bibliographical references, suitable material can be found to study these and other instruments.

3.3 Health education

The next step in working with families is, through proper communication, initiate a health education process that leads to the development of self-care and healthier lifestyles [6, 16]. Constructing a moment of health education and anticipation of situations that allows the family and the patient to understand the process of becoming ill and how this can impose changes and restrictions on their lives is one of the central points of the professional primary health care.

One of the key moments in introducing concepts of health education is when the family or the patient seeks the health team to solve a problem. At this moment, an adequate explanation about the process of becoming sick that gave rise to the demand takes the client in a very receptive situation to deal with the information. This is, in fact, one of the principles of adult education—adults only learn new knowledge when they make sense in their lives.

At this stage, it is necessary to remember that culture is not something learned only in schools, but the living and doing of the population are also expressions of it, and that to perceive this culture is the best way to promote any change that is intended to develop. The limit is given by the community itself, which has its parameters and beliefs, on which the professional should work. In order to promote any change, it is necessary to level the information to the customer's perception capacity, help him to perceive the situation, allow him to take the step of growth, and only then provide new data or present them with greater complexity. Health professionals are often seen blaspheming the community for not following their guidelines and thus not improving their health status. These professionals forget that it is not the community's lack of capacity to listen to them that hinders them but their own inability to give meaning to the information they wish to convey.

Working health education is the initial step for the community and its sick members to change their focus and habits in dealing with illness or risk situations to get sick. Since it implies a change of habits and attitudes, this education must be based on the history and experience of the people that one wishes to benefit. This is one of the fundamental principles of "working with families," because the basic goal is to help them find their ways and promote healthier lifestyles. The strategy of this education is to pay attention to the information that the community brings us, valuing the "tips" that are said in a veiled way and respecting the power lines of the community. If, for reasons of lack of training or fears of going into certain subjects, these moments are lost, the opportunity to provide alternatives is lost. Not realizing influential people in the community and how they see and deal with health issues will often lead to opposition from the proposals put forward. The correlation of forces, in most cases, is unfavorable to health teams.

3.4 Facilitation

Another basic element of working with families is the facilitation of communication among their members, a task that requires an adequate understanding of the family hierarchy and the way the group presents itself [6]. According to systemic theory, people tend to maintain, through their negative control mechanisms, the rules and positions they occupy in the structure. This often leads to communication blockages, which form the basis of stressful situations triggering the process of becoming ill. The primary care professional, because of his unique position in the community, can identify these blocks and through programmed actions allow an adequate exchange of information and feelings that facilitate the maintenance and recovery of the family health under study.

One of the great keys to the success of communication facilitation is the FIRO tool, which allows us to perceive the structure of families and their power relations and exchanges of feelings. With this knowledge, it is possible to identify the allies and impediments for communication to flow, as well as the determinants for the perpetuation of pathogenic situations. Always remembering the systemic theory, communication can be stimulated by participating in the communication rings of the family, discussing the determinants of the life processes of that family group and making an arc of reflection in which they perceive where they come from, where they are, and where they will go. This arc of communication projects the family a sense of unity and direction, allowing the health team to be valued as a link to foster family growth, gaining credibility and efficiency in health promotion.

Communication in situations of illness or conflict requires the primary care professional to take care of the perception of feelings of guilt and the situations of balance that the group presents. An interesting strategy may be the assembly of familiar sculptures, where the team reproduces the family grouping in a stylized way, trying to see who is leaning on whom and how the modifications can produce disturbances in the dynamics of the family group. Working with families is rewarding but requires professional dedication and commitment. The lack of perception of the family dynamics can compromise the effect of the intervention and lead to unsatisfactory results in family communication, without the expected improvement of the process. Situations of serious illness or impending death tend to put the family in a great stress, with the communication being made in a choppy way and filled with guilty silences. The work of facilitating communication enables people to explore their feelings and clarify their doubts, reducing the "silence pact" that is associated with depression and the worsening of pre-existing illnesses.

The construction of this proposal involves the discussion of the framework, with respect to hierarchies and lines of communication of the family, considering their taboos and without failing to clarify the process and the causal agents of the process. Important people in the family structure, even if not belonging to the grouping, should be invited to participate in the process so that the communication reaches the desired level of exchange. This avoids the persistence of shadows in the communication, which can make it less satisfactory. The attitude of the professional during these family gatherings should be to stimulate the exchange of feelings and expectations between the components, in order to facilitate the interaction and to clarify the doubts that exist about the pathology and its progression and the available treatment alternatives for the case.

3.5 References

In cases where it is necessary to refer the family or their patient to more complex levels, the technique of working with families also proposes a more interactive way: the reference is made explaining the reasons why the case is being addressed and which one's results are expected from this reference. In addition, contact is made with the referenced professional in order to accompany the patient and give subsidy on the situation experienced by the family during illness. This communication process increases satisfaction with referral, in addition to allowing more satisfactory results, because it gives confidence to the patient and his family, guarantees information to the reference professional, and enables the primary care professional to follow up the case on a continuous basis. This follow-up also allows for the clarification of the results obtained with the consultancy, in clearer terms to the patient and his/her family.

A final characteristic well emphasized by Papp [17] is teamwork. The view of several professionals about a given situation allows a better perception of the case under study, guaranteeing a broader vision and a result closer to the aspirations of the community. The shared look glimpses the various faces of the familiar kaleidoscope, which facilitates the understanding of the process of becoming ill, increases the capacity of identification of community resources to support the case in question, and prevents pathological attitudes in the relationship of a professional with the family group.

4. Genogram

In follow-up and family studies, understanding their natural history and patterns of illness may potentiate the action of health professionals. In this way the need arises to be able in a simple and objective way to create an instrument that shows graphically the structure and the pattern of repetition of the familiar relations.

This instrument is developed in North America to facilitate the understanding of families, based on the model of the heredogram, therefore called "genogram." Its basic characteristics are to identify the structure of the family and its pattern of relationship, showing the diseases that usually occur—the repetition of the patterns of relationship and the conflicts that lead to the process of becoming ill.

The instrument, useful to the health team, can also be used as an educational factor, allowing the patient and his/her family to have a sense of the repetitions of the processes that have been occurring and how they are repeated—facilitating the insight necessary to follow up the therapeutic proposal to be developed.

As long as the family has been drawn, they can realize its connections, strengths, and the pitfalls presented by their history, a very useful tool to start a communication process and to build up partnership.

5. Development of the family and the individual from the systemic perspective: family and individual life cycle and the impact of the illness

The systemic perspective for individual and family development is based on the concept of the life cycle, formulated by the sociological theory of the family, where the family life cycle and the individual life cycle fit together through interrelations of circularities and recurrence.

According to Graham [2], the family systems development model emphasizes changes in the developmental cycle of the family and individual life cycle, introducing a very important perspective in understanding the events of family life.

The concepts of ecology and the modern orientation of biology comprehend these developments in an interrelational and interdependent way, building maps of intersubjective for understanding the family and its members. Graham [2] highlights an important lesson of the ecological view "that no matter how conscious we may be, and how our actions may be deliberate, our acts become a part of a pattern whose form and effect generally exceed our understanding. An important point is that if this change happens within each individual and its subsystems, it will produce second-order changes that will, in the process of intercommunication, reverberate throughout the whole system, producing a kaleidoscopic rearrangement of each member."

In the systemic perspective, family and individual relational life is mediated by the passage of time and in the biological-social-cultural-psychic-political developments and transformations arising from this complex phenomenon.

Hoffman (in Graham) [2] argues that development is not a continuous process but characterized by transformations, second-order changes, and sudden emergence of simply nonexistent, more functionally organized patterns.

Not being considered in a linear fashion, as concatenated cause and effect events, the development of the family and the individual incorporates the notion of the dynamic interrelationship and the processes of recursion and equifinality for elements that belong to complex systems.

Graham states that "The family life cycle is not a linear event, it does not begin with a phase nor end with the deaths of members of a specific generation. Indeed, because death can happen at any stage in the family life cycle, it is not an event of life cycle but a life-changing event. That is to say, death is an event that happens within the context of the life cycle and can affect its evolution profoundly" [2].

Proposals on the definition and identification of family and individual life cycles contribute to the development of understandings about bio-psycho-social-cultural events in these moments of change, with the concept of crisis as a propelling event for cycle changes.

The energy of the crisis is understood in these evolutionary models as a propulsive force, occurring when the previously efficient adaptive mechanisms are not enough to maintain the stability of all intra- and extra-familiar movements, being necessary the application of new resources for its internal restructuring.

According to Wynne [18] there is a methodological problem in the study of the family life cycle, which would be to not reach an agreement on the number of stages that should be recognized. According to this author, the family life cycle has been subdivided by different authors, between 4 and 24 stages.

The interrelational versatility of the human being is an efficient destabilizer for the normalizations; in this way, every age of family and individual development presents new possibilities for solving the continuous process of belonging and individuation, perpetuating the task of maintaining and producing our personal and family histories, so that new stages and crises are redefined and localized.

One of the proposals used is related to the inter- and intra-oscillations [2], between periods of family closeness, periods of naturalness and entanglement, non-problematic periods, and periods of family distancing. This author finds four oscillations during life about events in an individual's development: birth, childhood, adolescence, and adulthood.

It also emphasizes that from the perspective of the family as a system, it understands these oscillations as having the function of providing a basis for the practice of intimacy relations and ego updates, in experiencing different levels of maturity and in the different tasks that the individual develops in the family.

Another proposal is the one used by Monica McGoldrick and Bety Carter [12], emphasizing the importance of a growing and integrative expansion of cultural-social-political-gender-racial differences in the understanding and manipulation of the life-cycle concept.

"We are born into families, our first relationships, our first group, our first experience with the world, happen to and through our families, we develop, grow and hope to die within our family context. a socio-political culture, takes shape and movement involved in the matrix of the family life cycle." McGoldrick and Carter [12], p. 1.

The authors understand the phases of the American family: becoming an adult, leaving the house, becoming a couple, family with young children, transformation of the family during adolescence, casting the children and moving on, and families in the late stage. Each of these events is accompanied by emotional processes characteristic of their transition and by expected developments for the second-order changes necessary for family development.

Galano [19] proposes the understanding of the family and individual life cycle through complex epistemology, taking into account differences and regularities, promoting the idea of dialogic experiences with family and individual events and their significant pluricontexts.

In this way, it uses the intergenerational, multidimensional, and multicontextual contingencies for the management of the family and individual life cycle with all its constituent elements.

"Intergenerational because the evolution of the family interferes and disrupts all members, both the nuclear family that is being constituted and the family of origin of the couple. Pluridimensional because functions, roles, values, feelings are subject to change and these do not always occur in the same way at the same time. The moments of passage from one stage to another face conflicts of interest, both 'within' members and 'among' family members. Cultural, religious, moral, racial, ethical, socio-economic contexts". Galano [19], p. 223

In a study that is closer to our Brazilian reality, which is so rich in values and cultural characteristics, the research carried out by Cerveny and Berthoud [20], recognizing the singularities of our Brazil, makes a cut for the study of the life cycle by the middle-class family of São Paulo.

"We do not feel very comfortable when we talk about the Brazilian family, for example. The diversity of models, the breadth of the territory, the different settlements, the miscegenation, the immigrations, the monstrous socioeconomic differences that exist in our country make it difficult to the generalization of a Brazilian family. The impression is that we have many Brazilian families, which are not only defined geographically, but which suffer many other influences". Cerveny and Berthoud [20], p. 33

This author organizes the middle-class São Paulo family in four phases: the family in the acquisition phase, the adolescent family, the family in the mature phase, and the family in the last stage.

Through the temporal perspective, this instrument organizes and constructs the history of the family and the individual and makes the understandings about the changes caused by the impact of difficult circumstances experienced by the family and its members, which are better defined, according to the possibilities, functions, potentialities, and limitations of each phase.

The concept of life cycle is an extremely useful tool in understanding the intense complexity that surrounds the developing family and individual life and its interrelationships with the environment; I consider one of the central elements of the systemic theory, for understanding the developments of the family.

6. Working based on the family system

The development of the family and individual life cycle, in its interrelations with social, cultural, psychological, biological, religious, gender, and geographical circumstances, produces coping resources for crises whose purpose is to deal with the problem of disease by protecting the system of any threat in its interactive dynamics.

The understanding of family dynamics with the lens of systems theory makes it possible to understand the interactional phenomena through the Morin [21] complexity theory proposal, understanding in this way that there are several significant events in family and individual life that must be understood from a perspective of difference and belonging.

Illness is part of one of these complex family interactions, which mobilizes various sectors of our society and culture and causes intense transformations in family and individual life and throughout its life cycle.

"In the arena of physical disease, particularly chronic disease, the focus of concern is the system created by the interaction of a disease with an individual, family, or other biopsychosocial system. From a familial point of view, family system theory has to include In order to place the unfolding of chronic disease in a developmental context, it is crucial to understand the interweaving of three evolutionary lines: the disease the individual, and the family life cycle thinking in an interactive and systemic way at the interface of these three lines." Rolland [22], p. 143.

This author posits that a serious illness happens as a blow to the family and turns into a point of reference by constructing or revitalizing interactions, from this moment on. Some diseases dismantle the future predictability of family and individual life in terms of the medium and long term.

Families in their multigenerational relationships have had experiences with illness and loss and also use these experiences and beliefs as an aid and guide in coping with the disease in the present time.

In this way, clinicians and families need a more effective way to work in the field of clinical consultations, applied to the development of any disease, which makes it possible to look at the future in a more collaborative way by updating the actions developed in other moments of the cycle vital part of the family.

"A scheme that conceptualizes chronic diseases and their relevance to psychosocial interactions is necessary, introducing into the biological world a common metalanguage that transforms or reclassifies the usual biological language. Chronic diseases need to be reconceptualized to some extent, this would organize the similarities and differences of the course of the disease, so that the type and degree of demands relevant to psychosocial research and clinical practice is highlighted in a more useful way." Rolland [22], p. 145

Rolland proposes for this planning the need for coevolutionary understanding of three structures: the disease, the individual, and the life cycles. It is necessary to consider the changes that occur, through the intercommunication between the life cycles in the family and individual life.

In the systemic understanding of this model, there is an interaction between the structures, the disease, the individual, and the family life cycle. Two main concepts are important for a more objective understanding of this interaction: the life cycle already discussed above and the structure of life.

By structure of life, Rolland understands as being those underlying patterns that are taught and form the family, the way they live and how does the family function at any point in the life cicle. Its main components include profession, love affairs, marriages in the family, functions coordinated by the family in various social situations, relationships between individuals and individuals with themselves, and the helper functions. The family life structure forms a barrier between the family and its members and the environment governing and mediating their relationships.

The structure of life is present throughout the life cycle and attaches importance to significant events during the changes required in each phase.

The key issue is that there is the notion of development in the life cycle sequence, including individual, family, and disease structure. This will have great influence of the cultural, socioeconomic, gender, ethical and racial diversity context.

To systematically think about the interface of these three lines of development, a common language and the organization of some concepts to be applied are necessary, considering the three structures simultaneously.

Two main steps are based on this model: (1) The need for a bridge between the biomedical and psychosocial worlds, a language that allows the chronic disease to be characterized in terms of psychosocial and longitudinal, and each of these conditions has specific characteristics and during the vital cycle appears with different demands. (2) Need to think simultaneously about family and individual development.

Rolland believes that a major impact on the relational life of the couple and their lives occurs in the event of a chronic illness. It proposes the family systemic model for work with diseases in interface with families and individuals. It is also a preventive work, which offers a framework for assessment, intervention, and support for families who are involved in the problem of chronic disease and living conditions being threatened.

This model is based on the systemic interaction between family and disease throughout the time. A good relationship between the demands of the disease and the family style of functioning and capacity building of the family are important determinants for the success or the location of dysfunctional resources and difficulties of adaptation.

Rolland points to the interface scheme between chronic disease and family and states that the variation of family conditions include the family and individual life cycles, the relationship with the life cycle and the stages of the disease, multigenerational legacies referring to the disease and loss, and the belief system. Not believing that it is possible to understand all the factors that compose the chronic disease problem and the family life cycle through the medical model emphasizes the intense importance of the social context of diseases and disabilities.

Family experience of illness and disability is strongly influenced by the dominant culture and health system affected by this culture.

In these conditions, he cites the incidence of diseases, the course of illnesses, the question of quality of life, and several other causes of suffering as produced by social discrimination. In the less privileged groups, it states that chronic diseases may be more prevalent and may occur earlier and in a more intense way, with a more difficult course due to problems with medical care and limited access to treatments.

Due to the technological advance, one can live a lot with a chronic illness, but this situation is often not experienced in the most deprived social strata, affecting both the family's capacity to organize resources for survival in prolonged periods of care and the individual development of its members in relation to all the demands produced by the chronic disease.

There are difficulties in integrating psychosocial work with traditional health services.

Today, many families can organize social network resources to help care for people with disabling problems, but never without spending extreme energy and effort, causing significant changes in their daily lives.

Rolland proposes the construction of a psychosocial typology of the diseases, organized in such a way that it contributes so that the family and clinicians have a form of understanding and action directed toward the integration of the preventive and curative structures.

These phases take into account the idea that diseases have a very significant temporal development peculiarity, just as each phase of the life cycle brings about the necessary relationships and behaviors, in the same way the disease in its development requires the mobilization of conduits within the cycle of individual and family life before healing or dead.

The first of these phases is the onset of illness: according to Rolland, diseases can be divided into those that occur suddenly and those that appear gradually, such as Alzheimer's disease. For sudden illnesses, emotional changes and more practical behaviors are required in a very short time, requiring the family a fairly rapid mobilization in the management of skills. Families who can tolerate explosive affective discharges, flexibility in changing roles, problems solved efficiently, and using external resources have more advantages in dealing with sudden illnesses. Gradual onset diseases such as Parkinson's require a longer adjustment period.

The second phase is the course of the disease: the course of chronic diseases have three general forms of progressive development, constant or with sporadic episodes.

Progressively, the family encounters a member with a constant symptom, in which the disability occurs gradually. Rest periods are rare due to the demands of the disease. The family lives in an ongoing process of change of function and adaptation due to disease progression. Increased exhaustion and effort of caregiver members occur because of increased demand for disease symptoms, and often the inclusion of new caregivers should occur.

Family flexibility, in the sense of internal reorganization of functions and ability to use external resources, is an excellent feature.

With the constant course of the disease, the occurrence of any event is followed by a stable biological event, for example: heart attack or severe pain in the spine. After a recovery period, the chronic phase is characterized by a period defined by a deficit or limitation. Returns to phases can happen, but the individual and the families face semipermanent changes during the course of life, so the possibility of family exhaustion exists, no matter how much effort new functions demand over time.

Relapses, or acute episodes such as asthma or disk problems, are distinguished by periods of stability and acute reactions. Families may return to more stable periods, but the spectrum of relapse always remains. Relapses require families to have different attitudes toward the adjustment process. The family is called to order in periods of exacerbation of crisis brought about by the disease. The tension in the family system is caused by the frequency and transition between periods of crisis and normalcy and by the uncertainty of when a new crisis will occur.

The result in these circumstances is the profound psychosocial impact that chronic, fatal, or episodic disease causes in the course of life. The most crucial factor is when the disease can be a sign of fatality.

In the continuum of the history of the disease, there are those that do not affect the period of life as much as arthritis (at the other extreme, there are progressive and fatal diseases such as cancer metastasis) and, in the intermediate area and in a more unpredictable category, those that shorten periods of life, such as cystic fibrosis or heart attack, and those with the possibility of sudden death, such as hemophilia.

The major difference between these three structures for the family is the experience of anticipatory losses and the effects of these circumstances during family life.

The future expectation of loss may cause difficulties in the family with the management and control of future perspectives. The family is almost always struggling between maintaining intimacy and keeping the sick member away from the occurrences of family life.

Varied, expected emotional reactions are important and can distract the family in its role of maintaining actions to solve problems that would maintain family integrity. The family, prior to the death of the sick member, or their responses to the disease situation are difficult and can lead to ill-adapted interactions, thereby withdrawing the sick member from the problem-solving space and responsibilities previously obtained.

Isolation of the diseased limb occurs in these situations, and in most cases this situation is related to a lack of medical management to inform the family about possible management for the continued treatment of the disease. When the loss is imminent or certain, it provides a fertility of emotional reactions and familiar verbalizations. Being able to create relationships varies between overprotection and secondary gain for the sick member. This situation is more relevant in situations of juvenile diseases such as hemophilia and diabetes.

When disability occurs, it may involve cognitive impairment such as Alzheimer's disease, sensory impairment such as blindness, impairment of movement such as paralysis, impairment in endurance such as heart disease, mutilation such as mastectomy, and conditions associated with social stigmas such as AIDS. The type and timing of disabling illness imply significant differences in the degree of family stress. The combination of one or more disabilities requires the family's intense reorganization of functions.

In some diseases the disability starts less severe and can go slowly worse, which gives the family conditions to organize functions and gives the sick member participation in planning as well. Combining types of disease onset, course, outcome, degree of disability, similarities, and differences in psychosocial patterns and their demands are crucial to offer a good care.

The question of uncertainties, for Rolland, refers to the degree of predictability and unpredictability of each disease, the specificity of each path, and what will be its consequences; all these doubts produce in the family often interrelationships and constructions of ambiguous beliefs.

For diseases with an unexpected course such as multiple sclerosis, the resources that the family can develop or already have, and their ability to adapt, especially future plans, are delayed or can be redone due to anticipatory anxiety and the inconstancy of events.

Families who can build long-term perspectives and jointly work with uncertainty, sustaining hope, are more prepared to avoid risks of exhaustion or dysfunction. Frequency, complexity, and efficacy of treatment, all situations involving the hospital and the cause in the patient's care, as well as the frequency and intensity of symptoms, are important issues, differing for each disease in terms of their characteristics and which should be considered from an evolutionary and systemically oriented perspective.

In most discussions about resources to fight against cancer, disability management, or agreements with how to situate the disease in everyday life, the understanding of the disease appears through a static form rather than the perception of the disease having a process over time.

For Rolland, the concept of temporal phase for each disease enables the clinician and families to think longitudinally and understand chronic disease as a process, with situations that transpire over time and with expected limits, transitions, and changing demands.

Each disease presents distinct phases, with psychosocial demands, and the development of attitudes, concerns, and tasks that require effort and changes for the family. The main themes related to the natural history of the disease can be described in three major phases: crisis, chronic, and terminal.

Crisis phase includes any symptomatic period prior to diagnosis and the initial period of readjustment after diagnosis and initiation of treatment plan. This period brings together a significant number of skills and tasks that must be developed and/or already exist in the family and the sick member.

Rolland informs about some universal practices that must be learned to coexist with chronic disease problems: understanding and learning about coping resources for symptoms and disability, adaptation to the treatment site, and establishment of a productive working relationship with the treatment team. The family must create meaning for disease that maximizes a sense of competence. Family members must face the mourning of life they had before the disease appeared in their lives. They need to understand illness as permanent while maintaining a sense of continuity between their past and their future. They need to organize together coping resources for the eminent crisis situation. When the crisis is about to happen, they need to develop flexibility in the face of future projects and reorientation of dreams and hopes.

Chronic phase, whether long or short, is the period of the cycle between the initial diagnosis and the readjustment and construction of the family's actions for the care of the sick member, where the questions about death and terminal illness predominate. This area is marked by episodes of constant progress or episodes of change. It is the day to day with chronic illness, those difficult moments that drag on for months or years.

The family and patient must build coping reactions and/or use the strength they have in organizing permanent changes and organize attitudes and behaviors that lead to a more comfortable day-to-day life for all of their members. The family's ability to keep matters current with chronic illness is the key to living through this period. If the disease is fatal, it is a very dense, difficult period where the passing of days is slow and intense commotion. For progressive and debilitating chronic diseases, the family feels tired having to deal with an exhaustive and endless problem.

In the terminal phase, the inevitability of death becomes apparent and dominates family life. The family deals with issues of separation, death, mourning, and the question of the reconstruction of family life after the loss. A sign of good transition happens when the family succeeds in letting go, emotional opening, seizing the opportunity to share time together, talking about unfinished business, and saying goodbye. Decide with the sick person about situations or objects for the family to live better, how far medical conduct, about the death at home or at the hospice, and the wishes on the funeral. These conversations, in fact, should be made in advance if there are progressive illnesses.

Rolland calls the clinical transition the transitions in the phases of illness that refer to the periods lived at each moment and its consequences and circumstances. There are periods in which the family reassesses their competence in the period prior to illness, in view of the demands of the disease in the current phase. Situations that have not been resolved during the previous phase can hinder or block transitional phases. Families and individuals may get frozen in structures that have been built in unsatisfactory survival ratio.

Each period has its specific task independent of the type of disease. Each type of disease has specific supplementary tasks.

This way of understanding chronic illness and family impact, through the choice of the systemic model, produces very useful clinical implications because it facilitates understanding and intervention in families with serious health problems along with the possible psychosocial disorders that accompany these circumstances.

Rolland draws attention to the following questions related to the characteristics of the diseases: aspect at the beginning of the illness, course, results and consequences, and inability. Acute diseases require a high level of adaptation, problem solving, function reorganizations, and balanced cohesion. Under these circumstances, helping families to maximize flexibility may be an important therapeutic interaction for a more satisfactory adjustment.

Each period of a disease delineates a characteristic type of psychosocial development; each phase has the development of its own abilities. It is important for families to be informed of their successes and know how to recognize them, to maximize the continuum of adaptations in the daily life of chronic diseases. Attention to the period and its requirements helps clinicians to access family strength and vulnerability in relation to the present and future stages of the disease.

These actions clarify the treatment plan by locating family characteristics relevant to the type and stage of the disease, sharing the information with the family, and helping to build objectives in a realistic way, giving the family a sense of power in their care journey of a member with chronic disease. Producing a pedagogical interaction with the family about the important signs of the illness, and re-orientation of the objectives in the treatment if necessary.

Rolland advises on the conditions of the family and the resources they have available if they combine with the transition points of the life cycle of the disease. Helping to approach the illness and the person who suffers it, and to develop an economic planning in terms of prevention.

During family living with the disease situation, it is extremely important to take into account, according to Rolland, the family beliefs about the meaning of the disease for the family, the family medical plan in a crisis situation, the family's ability to conduct in-home treatments, family communication when disease-oriented, problem solving, the reorganization of function, emotional involvement, social support, and the use and feasibility of social support.

For Rolland, the transition phases are the most vulnerable, because previous structures of the family, individual, and disease life cycle can be reintroduced in the form of new developmental tasks, which requires greater discontinuity in interactions rather than minor changes.

Often illness and disability tend to force the process of individual and family developments into transition and increased cohesion.

For example, in the period of education of children, if a disease happens at this stage, or shortly after this stage, a derailment may occur in the natural course of family development. A disease or disability in young or adolescent adults can develop relationships of extreme dependence and return the family cycle to the childhood care phase. The construction of autonomy and independence is in danger.

Parents need to review their plans in the social sphere to organize more care in the care of the sick person. As disease occurs in certain stages of the life cycle, it is likely that this moment may suffer from an extension in its manifestation.

When the disease appears in one parent, their ability to stay in course in the development of care and interaction with their children is severely affected.

In a more serious situation, the impact of the disease is like the arrival of a new child in the family, who has special needs and will compete with the children present; this situation can cause quite significant psychosocial changes, interfering in obtaining resources for help.

The illness captures the sick parent, and his relationship with the children is compromised. In many cases the family does not have the resources to function simultaneously with the demands of the disease and with the care of the children.

Often older children are called to share responsibilities along with other family members. All of these structural changes may be familiar supportive features, and clinicians need to be careful not to pathologize these interactions.

In this way, there is an intense interaction between the characteristics of the diseases, the circumstances in which they appear in the family and individual life cycle, and the consequences affecting all involved in this context.

Severe antisocial behaviors may occur more in adolescents, in the form of reactive or more constant peaks, worsening school performance, and reactions of isolation with the pairs of friends and with the members of the family; there may also be beneficial situations such as reorganization of sibling functions, increased sense and belonging and responsibility, restructuring in family relationships for more beneficial and rewarding interactions.

Qualifying and monitoring the solutions found by families is one of the great therapeutic resources in the follow-up of families with chronic, disabling, or fatal illnesses.

7. Social network

In the same way that illness and situations of extreme family and individual vulnerability cause suffering to the person and their significant family members, these situations also cause loss of reference in the community and society.

Systemic theory comes in the rescue of all cultural (wich look at relations, communication, and believes), communitarian, social, economic, religious, experienced and transmitted by families and their members for generations, and after transformed through the creative process in actions in the world for the development of the process of living. These singularities lost during this process of paradigmatic domination are rescued and qualified by the network concept.

For Sluzki [14], the 1990s were an evil decade, a time of medicalization of emotions. The repercussions of this model will be present in a deep and continuous way in this health/hospital interface; the effort of including the practice of interlacing relationships is daily, in all dimensions of this context, from the research to the administrative area.

Sluzki [14] defines network as the sum of all relationships that an individual perceives as meaningful or differentiates them as belonging to their interrelational context. This network corresponds to the interpersonal niche of the person and contributes substantially to his own recognition as an individual and to his self-image (**Figure 1**).

The network is formed by virtuous circles, having the function of protecting the health of the individual, and, consequently, the health of the individual maintains the social network. It is also formed by vicious circles where the presence of a family difficulty substantially affects the social network of the family and its individual members, a retraction in the maintenance of interactions with the significant community, and in the same way, this detachment appears in the network environment, occurring a process of reciprocal retraction.

According to Vasconcellos [25], the network provides sustenance support for families and individuals; for this author, the network is a distinction of the observer and, in this way, constructs spaces of interventions very useful in health work, because it expands the field of observer's view of the effects and limits of team performance and includes other contexts in the planning of therapy: the families of the people being served and the resources of the community. Producing collaborative actions in this way.

The disease event in the individual and family life, with all the resulting multi-interventions, alters the daily structures minimizing the maintenance of the networks of these systems, due to the social isolation produced by some diseases that diminish the interrelated possibilities affecting the health processes of the family and individual.

"The presence of a disease especially in the case of a chronic disease, usually debilitating or isolating, has an impact on the interactions between the individual, his/her family and the wider social network through different interrelated processes." Sluzki [14], p. 81.

The disease, as an event that involves crisis emergencies, causes a temporary immobilization in people's capacity to produce new relationships and to maintain relationships as usual, reducing the quality of the network and also reducing the possibility of people reaching their goal of quality of life.

According to Sluzki [14], the disease has an aversive interpersonal effect, restricts the mobility of the sick person and his family, reduces the activation initiative of the social network, and reduces the possibility of generating reciprocity behaviors.

A dramatic moment as a disease can generate virtuous circles in the already existing individual and family network, in the co-construction of new networks between families, sick people, health staff, and spaces in the community and society composed of people with capacity both material and emotional.

Sluzki [14] stresses that social support is the raison d'être of numerous self-management and self-help groups of patients and families suffering from chronic physical or emotional disorders; partial hospitalization or day hospital programs contain as one of its most important components the possibility of fostering the development and consolidation of a stable network of informal relationships and the learning or relearning of the skills needed to establish, nurture, and maintain active social relationships.

According to Vasconcellos [25], the network reduces the stress caused by the diagnosis, increasing a cycle of healthy feedbacks, not a vicious cycle of isolation and stigmatization, distancing, social asymmetry, and weakness.

Vasconcellos also points out that network maintenance effort is responsible for a system's resiliency capability. Work across the network values contextual and multi-contextual content, qualifying differences, enabling interacting people to become learners through situations that occur between people and the reported experiences of conflict resolution experienced.

8. Evaluating a family with the FIRO model

The disease is the consequence of a series of factors, involved with people's life choices and their genetic background and living conditions [5, 15]. Communication plays a fundamental role in human relationships, and it has a fundamentally self-referential view—and we always communicate [23]. So when the illness happens, a reflection is needed, "why does this happen at this moment?" "What leads to the emergence of this specific situation?" And still more the question: "how can we help this person or this family to find a better way to deal with your challenges?"

Schutz [24] in 1958 proposed the FIRO model (Fundamental Interpersonal Relations Orientation) for the study of small groups. In 1984 Doherty [24] adapts this model to systemic health care. According to Schutz the groups can be studied in three dimensions, namely, inclusion, control, and intimacy. Years later he rewrites about the method, and in 1977 he describes FIRO B—in which he develops work scales for group study.

8.1 Inclusion

When you are part of a group, the first question to be resolved is to be accepted by it; as long as we do not feel part of the group, we are going to act insecurely and generate attitudes so that they see, perceive, and recognize us. In a family this is also critical. The more I feel part and important, within the family nucleus, the more I feel free and able to fully develop within this context.

But it is not enough to be in the family; it is important that the space and the forms of communication are clear and acceptable so that I feel included. Doherty [4] raises the need to perceive what space and role we occupy within the family structure—and using Sluzki's framework [14], we can say that the more central we are within the family structure, the more knowledge we have about the rule and family designs for its members. Wilson [7] poses the issue of communication and subliminal issues—which often cloud our view of communication occurring within the family. And yet in this item, questions about how we share acts and things make the complexity of this component.

The issue of inclusion is so impotent that it is a cornerstone in the systemic structural therapy proposed by Minuchin [9]. And how does inclusion work? Before interacting in a particular group, you need to know what our space and what capacity for influence we have. A child tests boundaries uninterruptedly to find out this, teenagers question rules and limits family and adults try to assert their positions—all this is inclusion, but not just this.

The agreed rules in each group are part of this component, where issues often escape the external observer and will only become apparent with systematic pursuit—family secrets, entrenched beliefs about health issues, and accepted or non-accepted behaviors. So detailing in a map of questions about what and how the person and his family perceive the health situation makes us able to better understand their positions and provides the appropriate condition to propose valid interventions. The family's communication style and the way they determine their roles and functions within the family provide a very rich material to be worked on.

8.2 Control

The second component of the FIRO model is control, and it is the second component because without knowing its space and being accepted in a certain group, it is impossible to have some type of control. The exercise of control can be done in different ways—direct and indirect—and will depend on the family structure and its power lines.

When assessing a family, the observer often has difficulty understanding the chains of command, which are exercised either by economic power, personal leadership, or structural family issues. When entering within the scope of the family, it is basic to discover how it reacts to situations of stress and of the decision processes, because the different types of control become apparent.

Classically Wilson [8] divides the control into dominant, collaborative, and reactive. But the nuances of these components are more complex and require special attention from the observer. Dominance may be in some areas, and the way of exercising it varies greatly, with different results. The same goes for the other modes of control.

The understanding of these behaviors shows its importance in the adhesion of the patients to the different treatments, particularly when talking about chronic disease. Dominant people within a social nucleus if they do not understand the pathology and the proposal of intervention can hinder adherence to the treatment and the changes of the necessary habits.

Some family therapy schools base their actions on this component, such as the strategic school developed by Haley.

8.3 Intimacy

The third component proposed by Schutz is intimacy. When I recognize myself as part of a group, I know my place, and I have some kind of control within it; I am ready to establish exchange relationships, and I am able to share emotions and feelings.

More subtle within the work centers, the knowledge of affective relationships and loyalty is a powerful way to gain adherence and support the people to whom attention is given.

Also some family therapy schools are based on this component as the humanistic school of Satir.

Working on it is simple. The model was designed for working with groups within social settings; the adaptation proposed by Doherty [5] and later by Wilson [8] brings the tool to the family and supports the treatment of family and support for clinical interventions.

The instrument can be used in individual care by taking a person-centered approach. In this context the approach explores the knowledge it has about the health situation and how this is influenced by its environment. How much of their autonomy is affected by the situation, who defines the searches and priorities of care and the changes and treatments to be performed. Finally with whom in the group he/she shares his/hers doubts and complaints.

Used in this way, the FIRO is simple and broadens the dialog, favoring adherence to the treatment besides narrowing the patient doctor relationship.

In situations where changes are difficult, people have difficulty adhering to treatment or the results fall short of the goals proposed the use of a family interview with the support of the methodology can be very useful.

In these cases, the interviewer should listen to all members and care about absent members, or who refuses to participate is crucial because they generally play an important role within the family structure and may render the approach ineffective. An interviewer considering FIRO should listen to the family's understanding of the health situation, their beliefs, and previous experiences with similar situations. Next identify the key people in the family hierarchy—providers, tasks and spaces of each member, forms of communication, and people who are considered "scapegoats" of the family.

At a later moment, one can seek to explore the power lines within the family, identifying who actually decides and how people collaborate or resist the proposals of people who have some control within the family. This will identify how the family facilitates, or creates, difficulties in controlling the case.

Example: attending a family with diabetes and the generally inadequate control generated a family interview to understand the difficulties in following the guidelines regarding lifestyle habits and therapeutics. It became obvious that the family greatly valued the use of the drugs that were used properly, with the consumption monitored by the team as planned. But the person who made purchases and took responsibility for food had a low understanding of what diabetes would be, as well as feeding a person with the disease. During the approach it was made clear to all that food would always have sugars and that the fractionation of the diet and the use of foods with slower release of sugar would be fundamental to the control. The target patient of the activity put how much she felt taken care of by the relatives, who did many things for her—but also did not perceive clearly the dietary error. After the interview there was a 30% reduction in glycemic levels, without the family losing the affective link and improving the understanding of the health team's concerns about the patient on the screen.

The use of FIRO can be taken to improve care by inviting people, families, or groups to talk about the dimensions in which the instrument was studied—people are invited to talk about themselves and to perceive themselves within their context. This improves understanding of the processes and by itself is already therapeutic.

The professional who understands the dimensions of belonging, control, and intimacy can transform the dialog with patients in a process of growth and review of situations, which makes the interview rich and motivating. The key question is, the perception of how central to each element is how your life is organized, how it perceives the interpersonal relationships in your group, and how it influences their lives.

For most people, exchanging information in a quiet dialog can reshape their sufferings and difficulties without requiring any intervention by the therapist—only the flow of dialog and openness to encourage people to talk about their expectations and difficulties within the relationship.

By understanding the concept of a biopsychosocial model, it is clear that a group interactions are an important part of the health-disease process. By establishing a thoughtful conversation, people begin their journey of recovery.

9. Conclusion

A family system approach is now a concept that is well developed and, despite its challenging way to think, allows the health professional to have an open, broad comprehension of the context. Based on that, it is possible to help people to better understand their situation and find a new path to have a healthier life.

Most of the time, the blindness attached to a lack of comprehension of the facts linked to any situation is the cause of suffering and may be one of the key points to the development of any ill that will emerge in the future.

This approach to families turns blindness into understanding and can be a pathway for the development of new languages among families and health professionals. New indicators of well-being would be recognized by increasing the quality of life of families and communities.

Author details

Hamilton Lima Wagner[1,2]* and Tania Dalallana[3]

1 Health System of Curitiba, Curitiba, Brazil

2 Family and Community Medicine of Curitiba, Curitiba, Brazil

3 Federal University of Paraná, Curitiba, Brazil

*Address all correspondence to: hamiltonw@uol.com.br

References

[1] Khun TS. A estrutura das revoluções cintíficas. 5th ed. São Paulo: Perspectivas; 1997

[2] Lee C-G. A developmental model for family systems. Family Process. 1985;**24**:139-150

[3] Grassano S et al. Abordagem Sistêmico Integrativa. Curitiba: CD Rom—Chaim; 1996

[4] Stewart M et al. Medicina centrada na pessoa. 2nd ed. Porto Alegre: Artmed; 2010

[5] Cristiee-Seely J. Working with Families in Primary Care. New York: Kellogg's Foundation; 1984

[6] Talbot YR. Family System Medicine. Toronto: Publicola Geg'd; 1991

[7] Freire P. Pedagogia da Esperança. Rio de Janeiro: Paz e Terra; 1992

[8] Wilson L. Trabalhando com famílias—livro de trabalho para residentes. Curitiba: Secretaria Municipal de Saúde de Curitiba; 1996

[9] Minuchin S. Famílias Funcionamento & Tratamento. Porto Alegre: Artes Médicas; 1990

[10] Wagner ABP, Wagner HL, Talbot Y, Carmo AE. Aplicação de Rede Social no Manejo da Hipertensão. Vol. 1. Curitiba: RBMFC; 2004

[11] Wagner HL et al. Ferramenta de Descrição da Família e dos Seus Padrões de Relacionamento—Genograma—Uso em Saúde da Família. Vol. 57(1/2). Curitiba: Revista Médica do Paraná.; 1999. pp. 28-33

[12] McGoldrick M, Carter B, editors. The Expanded Family Life Cycle: Individual, Family and Social Perspectives, USA. 3rd ed. Allyn & Bacon; 1999

[13] Wagner HL et al. Ferramenta de Avaliação Para Situações Indefinidas e Manobras Preventivas em Saúde da Família—Ciclo de Vida das Famílias. Vol. 57(1/2). Curitiba: Revista Médica do Paraná.; 1999. pp. 22-27

[14] Sluzki CE. La Red Social: Frontera de la practica sistemica. Barcelona: Gedisa; 1996

[15] Wagner HL. Avaliação Familiar. PROMEF. Artmed. Ciclo 7. Vol. 2. 2012

[16] Freire P. Pedagogia da Autonomia. 43rd ed. São Paulo: Paz e Terra; 2011

[17] Papp P. O Processo de Mudança. Porto Alegre: Artes Médicas; 1991

[18] Wynne L et al. Professional Politics and the Concepts of Family Therapy, Family Consultation And Sistems Consultation. Vol. 26. Fam Pro; 1988

[19] Galano MH. O ciclo vital da família uma visão complexa. In: Perspectivas Psicodinâmicas em Psiquiatria. São Paulo: Lemos; 2001

[20] Cerveny MOC, Berthoud EMC. Família e Ciclo Vital: Nossa realidade em pesquisa. São Paulo: Casa do Psicólogo; 1997

[21] Morin E. Introdução ao Pensamento Complexo. Porto Alegre; 1999

[22] Rolland J, Families S, editors. Illness and disability. An Integrative Treatment Model. New York: Basic Books; 1994

[23] Watzlawick P, Beavin JH, Jackson DD. Pragmática da Comunicação Humana. São Paulo: Cultrix; 1973

[24] McDaniel SH et al. Terapia Familiar Médica. Porto Alegre: Artes Médicas; 1994

[25] Esteves de Vasconcellos MJ. De sistemas, redes e paradigmas. In: Anais do III Congresso Brasileiro de Terapia Familiar: O individuo, a família e as redes sociais na virada do século. Rio de Janeiro: Asociação Brasileira de Terapia Familiar e ATF-RJ; 1998

Section 2

Improving Children's Future

Chapter 4

The DAVAd: A Narrative Tool to Explore the Early Stages of the Adoptive Bond

Barbara Cordella, Paola Elia, Marzia Pibiri and Alessia Carleschi

Abstract

The DAVAd (the first bond process diary) is a new narrative tool created to accompany the adoptive couple during their trip to the land of the child/children to whom they have been matched. The tool presented is the first to explore what happens, in term of events and emotional experiences, during the first meetings between the parental couple and the child/children. This period is clinically relevant as the ideal is compared with the real. The DAVAd supports the parental couple in focusing on their experiences and their meanings and learning to deal with the complexity related to the bound construction. Moreover, the DAVAd allows the clinical psychologist in detecting and treating, if necessary, the familiar dynamics, favoring the prevention of the distress. A clinical case that utilizes the DAVAd will be presented, to enlighten the way its compilation can be used by researchers and clinicians.

Keywords: adoptive bond, international adoption, narrative diary, adoptive parent-child first meeting, post-adoption

1. Introduction

The method to investigate the phenomenon of international adaptation has progressively changed over the years. There has been a shift from a perspective that was meant to legitimize mostly the needs of the parental couple to a perspective aimed at safeguarding children's rights; later on a new perspective was developed that regards the adoptive family as a *system* to be protected and supported. In other words, there has been a shift from an extremely optimist outlook, which considered the adoption the best solution for children, biological parents, and the adoptive couple, to a more realistic approach, which regards adoption as an opportunity but at the same time acknowledges the challenges and the issues the people involved in the adoption process have to face [1].

The Hague Convention of 29 May 1993 on Protection of Children and Cooperation in Respect of Intercountry Adoption certainly drove this change of perspective. The convention recognized that the child should grow up in a family environment, thus promoting the adoption of children with special needs and/or school-age children and making adoptive families face specific difficulties and issues. It is widely acknowledged that when children have been in the child welfare system for long periods or have a background of abuse and neglect, those conditions may cause developmental delays, interfere in the relationship with the new caregivers, and represent a risk factor for adoption breakdown [2, 3].

If in the past, the adoptive family was considered to be on the same level of the biological family, thus neglecting its peculiarity, today we know that building an adoption bond is a complex phenomenon that may only safely be developed if the specific development challenges, involving adoptive parents, children, and the counsellors working with them, are acknowledged. Risk factors may be reduced by the relationship with the new family [4, 5], provided that its members are supported by trained counsellors and can benefit from dedicated services [6, 7].

However, Van IJzendoorn and Juffer [8] state that adoption is already a "curative intervention" and a "protective factor" (p. 1229) as it fulfills the desire of adoptive parents to have children and offer children a second chance to experience a family and emotional relationship and bond, which are essential to them.

Vadilonga [9] agrees with Van IJzendoorn and Juffer as he states that adoption represents a reparative effort and promotes the development of a multiple identity. He writes, "Children placed for adoption have specific problems and often show signs of post-traumatic stress disorder; in order to make the adoption process successful, it is essential that adoptive parents become the main point of contact in the reparative and working-through process of the child" (p. 34). This is possible if parents managed to "activate" their reparative capabilities, which mainly refer to the ability to listen, thus sharing a development process that allows the child to listen to himself/herself. Adoptive parents can therefore provide children with support, containment, and bonding and help them to reflect and process their own story [10].

In other words, the path to adoption can be therapeutic and trigger a transformation process, provided that the child is accompanied toward new relational experiences that may integrate the construction of the self and the representation the child has got of himself and the others. The answers of adoptive parents can confirm or discount the survival strategies children developed to handle with violent, untrustworthy, or absent caregivers.

From that point of view, both research and interventions should be focused less on the exclusive placement of the child with special needs and more on the care of the family system, the relationship between the child and the parents; the aim should be to support and promote a circular growth path, thus driving the development of patterns of relationship different from those learnt in the birth family background of the child [11]. A better awareness of the rights of adopted children and of the role played by adoptive parents as potential co-therapists helped to turn the attention on the training of adoptive parents but also on the need to develop preliminary and continuous interventions.

2. Research on adoption breakdowns

Research carried out with the aim of quantifying and understanding the phenomenon of adoption breakdowns can be useful to the purpose of this study to the extent that it offers information to rethink support to adoptive families.

The main references will be made to what is stated by Vadilonga [9], in his book published in 2010, and to what is recommended by Paniagua, Jiménez-Morago, and Palacios [12] with regard to their research carried out on adoption breakdowns in Spain, over the decade 2003–2012, and presented in Milan in 2016. Further reference will be made to the Italian research carried out by the Commissione per le Adozioni Internazionali (CAI), in collaboration with the Istituto Innocenti [13], and the literature review carried out by a team at the University of Minnesota [14]. Even though the research reviewed is not recent, it is the only one available on a topic not easy to analyze.

In literature, authors agree on the fact that the phenomenon of adoption breakdown is the result of multiple risk factors coexisting and regarding three main players: the parental couple, the child, and the counsellors and adoption professionals working with the family. With regard to children, several risk factors were identified. The most important of them is the one connected to late adoption [14]. However, the research carried out by Paniagua and his colleagues shows how the risk of adoption breakdown increases proportionately with the age of the adopted child only in the age bracket between 2 and 6 years old and that it cannot be the only risk factor explaining the adoption breakdown [12]. With regard to the parental couple, the same research identifies as a risk factor the low motivation and training of the parents. It is also interesting to observe that, both in Spain and Italy, there is reluctance among parents to ask for support so that it is advisable not only to develop further local support services but to drive a real change in the culture forming the background of the adoption process [15].

The authors agree that there is a low percentage of adoption breakdown, but estimates may vary depending on the source taken into consideration (from 1 to 1.8% [13]; from 1 to 7% [16]; from 1 to 32% [12]). The differences observed among the estimates may be due to the different areas investigated, to the difficulty to collect data, but also to the definition of adoption breakdown used. From a legal perspective, it is possible to distinguish between adoption disruption and adoption dissolution. The term disruption is used to describe an adoption process that ends before the adoption is legally finalized through the adoption order, while the term dissolution is used to describe an adoption process that ends after the adoption is legally finalized.

In both cases, however, all the difficult relationship patterns experienced as insurmountable by the main actors, that is, children and adoptive parents, which however are not the cause of a final separation are not taken into account. Those critical situations may be overlooked in the monitoring, if the families do not ask for help.

According to a research carried out by CAI, the number of adoption breakdowns is mainly the same in national and international adoption processes [17, 18].

Different research articles show how adoption breakdown happens during the adolescence or preadolescence of the adopted child in most of the cases, revealing signs of distress in the adoptive parent-child relationship that has been going on for years without being identified and treated. In those situations, as Vitolo [19] observes, the "rejection and pushing-away" behavior of adoptive parents seems to be aimed at distancing themselves from the child as well as from the anguish of feeling helpless.

In the interviews carried out with some children who experienced adoption breakdown [13], a common factor emerging seems to be the impossibility to acknowledge the other and be acknowledged by him/her, and such a distress may be shown even when children were adopted at a very young age. In those cases, according to Lombardi [20] what seems to lack is a "a mental space for the other and the bonding, which turns into the impossibility to experience a verbalized space and the inability to become beings experiencing relationships subject to change: the dysfunctional family (unlike the others) is blocked in that experience, not progressing but sticking in time to that feeling of 'non-belonging' around which the subsequent relationship is built" (p. 80).

Those results are connected to the opportunity to adopt a constructive approach to respond to adoption crises through two preventive strategies: the training of the parental couple before the adoption and first of all early detection of conflicts and problems and early intervention to support the "therapeutic" abilities of adoptive parents. The attention focused on the prevention and early support to parents makes attention also to be drawn on the first stages of the path to adoption, starting from the meeting between the child and the parental couple. Even though prospective parents were trained and their ability to manage conflicts and adjust to new and problematic situations was analyzed, it is in the face-to-face contact between the main players of the adoption that feelings of joy and acceptance but also misunderstandings and frustration can be experienced. Conflicts may become harsher, above all in the case of older children, who already have a well-defined personality and are less willing to give up the psychological strategies that have saved them from the despair of abandonment. At the same time, parents may develop defensive strategies unconsciously that make them afraid of their educational role, not self-confident, disappointed by the emotional distance of the children, and unable to deal with the developmental crisis and the necessary paths to mutual adjustment having a positive and constructive attitude. The presence of qualified counsellors as well as the early detection and management of distress may stop that potentially destructive process [21]. In other words, it is necessary to intervene before the development of deep-rooted mutual prejudices makes the parties impossible to know each other and "reach an agreement" [22].

3. Useful guidelines to develop the intervention

The research carried out and cited in the previous paragraph provides some guidelines for the development of further research and intervention in the matter.

In general terms, it seems necessary to drive a cultural change that, on the one side, allows adoptive families to turn to support services to receive the support they need in their path to adoption and, on the other side, allows services to look at adoptive families as a resource to be trained instead of subjects to be analyzed.

Throughout this path, it appears essential to focus the attention on the meetings between parents and children, both in the pre-adoption and post-adoption stages, in order to detect any problem, thus promoting the development of a "family system" rather than mutual incomprehension getting worse.

This would be possible if adoption professionals work with parents on their ability to narrate about themselves, recognizing and validating the feelings aroused by the relationship with adopted children, first imagined and later experienced, in order to promote the necessary learning that will allow the parental couple to accept the experience of life and behaviors of children.

Narrating the family relationship means to give oneself the opportunity to think about it, weakening, as Salvatore [23] emphasizes, "the sense of truth connected to the emotional building of the experience, offering the opportunity to explore different and additional ways of interpreting reality" (p. 68).

Such a line of development is further confirmed by psychoanalytic literature [24, 25], which studied the path to biological parenthood, from the preparation to the transition to parenthood. In the course of the pregnancy and when meeting the newborn, the parental representations play a crucial role as they will drive the type of emotional investment and the care quality the parents will provide to the newborn. The emotional and symbolic dimension of pregnancy, which is common to biological pregnancy and to the path to adoption [26], plays a key role in the psychological wellbeing of the family. It prepares and helps parents to develop their role as parents, allowing them to think about and mentally contain the child, identifying his/her needs that have to be met and separating them from their own needs [27].

In the case of adoptive parents, in addition to the development of their own role as parents and the acceptance of the history of the children, it is necessary to take into account the grief for failed procreation and the awareness of meeting a child who has already lived a part of his/her own story, probably affected by adversities [28]. It is easy to think that, on the other side, the child waiting for an adoptive parent will have his/her own feelings of anxiety and expectations. To the purpose of this study, this is regarded as important as international adoptions, which are today more frequent, involve school-age children. Based on the present knowledge, children's expectations are often hard to know, for both the adoptive parents and researchers, and may be revealed only at the time of the face-to-face contact; however, it can be said that this is not applicable to the expectations of adoptive couples.

For adoptive couples the meeting groups of parents who prepare themselves to meet a child to adopt have been long since recognized as essential.

The group plays a very important role because it allows peer comparison and the open discussion of parents' fantasies about the child and the first interactions with him/her [10]. In the groups, the verbalization of doubts, fears, and prejudices is explicitly favored in order to prevent reactions including rejection, detachments, and extreme defense against resistances or simply against what is unknown and cannot be predicted [29]. Prospective parents often daydream about their first meeting with the child, so long-awaited, thinking about it as an immediately acknowledgment of their own role as parents and that of the child, as a magic ailment to the wounds experienced by the child due to abandonment and by the couple for failed procreation [20]. As experiences show, it is a fantasy that helps to remove the effort for being involved in a new and demanding relationship, and it is therefore useful to have the space and time needed to analyze it.

With regard to the stage of face-to-face contact between adoptive parents/child, there is also a gap in the literature.

Although that stage of transition is regarded as highly important, with the identifications of the issues that may arise [30], there is no research analyzing the facts [31].

Our review of specialized literature only allowed us to find one article [29]: it is a qualitative study, based on the interviews of 46 parental couples who told about their meeting with the adopted minor. The limitation of the above mentioned article, however, is the time between the adoption and the interview, which ranged from 1 to 16 years. In the interviews carried out, the three topics most frequently discussed and which show a higher level of emotional intensity were the time when the child was officially placed into the custody of the adoptive parents, the discovery of his/her own body, and the first interactions. Different themes emerged were referred to those topics: the feelings of loneliness and anxiety felt at the time of the face-to-face contact, the shocking images of the life conditions of children, the lack of training to the contact with the child, the lack of information received about the child, the fear about his/her health conditions, the fear for reactions of the child such as rejection or aggression, and the contrast between the expected interaction and the one actually experienced.

The themes identified confirm the need to focus more on the stage of the first face-to-face contact, but in the literature there are no tools designed for this.

4. A new tool: the DAVAd

In the view of what is stated in the previous paragraphs, our research group developed a narrative diary, called DAVAd (Italian acronym for Diario di Accompagnamento del Viaggio Adottivo, translated as "first bond process diary"), which is a useful tool offered to couples, who chose international adoption, as a "companion" during their journey to the country of birth of the child they were matched to. This tools was designed with the aim of providing clinicians with a support tool to their work, "opening a window" on the first interactions between adoptive parents and children.

The tool offered to parents suggests them to narrate an episode regarded as meaningful one for each day they spent abroad, during which they experienced the relationship with their adopted children.

The diary follows the following narrative pattern:

- Introduction: place, time, people participating

- Event: what they decided to write on the diary

- Consequences: how the event terminated, what the parents learnt, the reaction of the child/children, etc.

After that, parents are asked to write down their emotions and the relevant level of intensity (very low, low, medium, quite high, very high, incredibly high), indicating whether those emotions refer to the father/mother and/or child.

The DAVAd therefore suggests a narrative framework, but it also gives parents the opportunity to tell about the episode freely. The focus, even with regard to emotions and feelings, is on the ability of the couple to acknowledge them, write them down, and state their level of intensity. The DAVAd is used to collect the narrative choices made by the couple, the way in which the parents tell the experience they are having. The focus is not on the collection of facts, rather on the identification of the strategies developed by adoptive parents and children at the beginning of their relationship.

4.1 Why a diary?

The proposal to write a diary or to use the narrative of the events as a tool is not something new (Daily diary methodology: Bolger et al. [32]; Gunthert and Wenze [33]; Lischetzke [34]). In the post-adoption context, autobiographical narrative is often used as a cognitive and reflection tool to save memories and make a family tale be organized more easily in order to support the construction of a bonding [35], legitimizing at the same time the need of each family member to feel part of the family but also to have his/her own story to tell [36].

More in general, narrative is thought to have a transformational value as it allows the experience and memories associated to it to be turned into a narrative form (e.g., Freud [37]; Bion [38]; Matte Blanco [39]; Bucci [40]). Giving a structure to that form means to organize communication in a consistent way, with a precise time and causal order, identifying and giving a name to the emotions felt, thus driving people to provide an interpretation of the events inevitably [41, 42]. According to this approach, narrative is considered also a tool that may help to overcome traumas and improve the psychophysical conditions of the narrators [43, 44].

In the case of the DAVAd, the narrative to be built can pursue even more specific goals, besides those already mentioned.

In particular, it is useful to underline its educational role, both on the levels of content and method.

On the level of content, it has to be pointed out that parents are suggested to write a diary during the only period of time they are alone, without their own cultural and personal reference points, in a foreign land. Thinking over their own experience of foreignness consisting of an environment made of smells, climate, cultural codes, language, habits, food, etc., different from their familiar ones, may help adoptive parents to understand what their adoptive children will experience once they will have left their country of birth and daily life. Therefore, this could help to develop the observation skills of prospective parents [45].

With reference to method, it has to be highlighted that the habit of writing a diary about the events related to the family relationship means to be able to stop and recollect what happened during the day and choose only one episode. Therefore, before starting writing, parents need to detach from the flow of events, thus building a particular material and mental setting. The act of writing the DAVAd can be considered a useful pretext to develop the ability to reflect on personal and relational daily dynamics.

Lastly, the act of writing a diary represents a meaningful act within the relation between the couple and the clinician working with them in the pre-adoption and post-adoption stages. The receipt of the DAVAd and its writing are acts proposed to make more present the background support provided by the counsellor in charge of managing the path to adoption: the diary can be regarded as a transitional object that reminds of the dialogue, temporarily interrupted, with the reference clinician. The episodes narrated will give the counsellor useful clues to understand how the narrative of the new family is being built, the criteria for interpreting and explaining events within the relationship, the type of reflexive ability used by the couple, and therefore what type of support should be offered to them later on.

4.2 The DAVAd and the reflexive function

Despite the observations made in the previous paragraph, the act of writing a diary can also be considered a very demanding effort for the couple. Even though such an issue needs to be taken into account, it also needs to be addressed when considering the specific role adoptive parents start to play during their journey. The act of writing requires an effort similar to the one the adoptive parent is going to make based on his/her new role as a parent.

This can be better explained as follows.

A child going through the path to adoption is a child who suffered from being separated from his/her birth family but who may have experienced other events that may be defined as traumatic ones. Those events affect the child's reflexive function [46], that is, the ability to interpret behaviors, personal and those of others, in terms of hypothetical mental states, be they thoughts, feelings, wishes, and intentions, thus promoting the building of (self and others') representations that are incompatible among themselves and are therefore left separated from each other [47].

For example, the feeling of having been inflicted an unfair punishment may lead to a representation of parents incompatible with that of a loving and caring parent. On the contrary, if the child is able to consider the unfair punishment not a result of his/her condition as a child not deserving love or of the cruelty of adoptive parents, experienced as absolute dimensions, but only as the result of a temporary condition, then it is possible to be able to reconnect the two different representations.

For the child the opportunity to regain a unitary model of the self and of the other is connected to the reflexive function of his/her new parents who can gradually make understandable and foreseeable the behavior of the self and of the others; this will reduce the needs to separate the representations and will promote the absorption of new relational experiences. As Bastianoni [48] observes "the entry of the child in the world of minds is almost a process of apprenticeship whereby caregivers encourage the child to adopt mentalizing concepts. The acquisition of a reflexive ability thus becomes part of an intersubjective process between the child and the caregivers" (p. 34).

If we look at this from the point of view of the couple, for example, the child is likely to have learnt dysfunctional patterns of relationships that are symptoms of the need to defend himself/herself and the inability to trust caregivers. This means that adoptive parents need to learn that a rejection behavior against them may be the expression of the child's fear to trust them but also the desire to meet them.

On the other side, the possibility to accept the life experiences of the minor, the "internal events" driving his/her behavior, is based on the parental ability to identify their own emotional states, recalled by the relationship, reflecting on them [49].

The DAVAd can therefore be a useful tool whose writing should be recommended to parents.

5. A case study

By way of example of what is stated above, the analysis of a DAVAd is hereby presented, which was written by a couple who left for a journey for the international adoption of two sisters, aged 8 and 9 in 2017. As researchers, we analyzed the written report using the same reading categories used during the observation of an interview, taking into account When, How, and What was "said" (see **Table 1**).

5.1 When

The first remark is about the days of diary writing. Even though the couple was given instructions to write the dairy every day, the act of writing is clearly and strongly irregular. Over a period of 30 days spent abroad, only eight episodes were reported. In addition to those episodes, five more were added when the family came back home and narrated over a period of 5 months. What is therefore analyzed is not a diary but a collection of episodes, which clearly points out the need to understand when the diary writing was regarded as appropriate.

5.2 How

In the 13 episodes narrated, no attention is paid to the field "Introduction," which is filled in with a more general reference to the place where the event occurred. The perception is that the episode narrated is regarded as a moment of discontinuity compared to their expectations or the normal flow of events. In other words, unexpected events seem to be narrated, which are hard to refer to the previous situation, in line with what is stated by Chafe [50], according to whom the need to narrate, to give consistency and continuity to one's own experience, is revealed only by what actually does not match with the expectations, that is, the incomprehensible and unexpected event. On the level of content, the hypothesis made is further confirmed by the repetition of the term "suddenly."

5.3 What: emotions

Figure 1 shows the emotions both parents list to have felt with reference to the episodes narrated.

It can be observed that helplessness and grief are the emotions most cited, together with fear, often described as the fear "of not understanding" and

When	How			What	
	Introduction	**Event**	**Consequences**	**Emotion**	**Event**
1st day of trip 13/06	X just the place	X		Mother: sorrow (5) Father: dejection (4), fear (2) Child 1: Child 2:	Leaving the institute
2nd day of trip 14/06	X just the place	X		Mother: tenderness (3) Father: tenderness (3) Child1: Child2:	Collaboration and jealousy of the girls
5th day of trip 17/06	X just the place	X	X	Mother: impotence (3), sorrow (3) Father: impotence (3), fear (3) Child 1: Child 2:	Whim of the oldest girl
9th day of trip 21/06	X just the place	X	X	Mother: impotence 5, confusion (4), sorrow (4) Father: impotence (4), confusion (4), sorrow (4) Child 1: Child 2:	Intolerance to frustration of older sister
18th day of trip 30/06	X just the place	X	X	Mother: fear (3) Father: fear (4) Child 1: Child2:	Whim of the oldest girl
20th day of trip 02/07		X		Mother: Father: Child 1: Child 2:	Nocturnal enuresis of the older sister
23th day of trip 05/07	X just the place	X		Mother : sorrow (5) Father: Child 1: Child 2:	Melancholy due to the lack of children who were in the institution
27th day of trip 09/07		X	X	Mother: sadness, sorrow Father: fear Child 1: despair Child 2: despair	Desperation for the removal of the mother
15/09 at home		X	X	Mother : confusion Father: Child 1: Child 2: rage	Provocation of the youngest child

When	How			What	
	Introduction	Event	Consequences	Emotion	Event
11/10 at home		X	X	Mother: confusion Father: Child 1: Child 2: rage	Provocation of the youngest child
5/12 at home		X	X	Mother: rage Father: Child 1: Child 2: rage	Provocation of the youngest child
10/01 at home		X		Mother: Father: Child 1: Child 2:	Nocturnal enuresis of the older sister
21/01 at home		X		Mother: sadness, impotence Father: sadness, impotence Child 1: sadness Child 2: sadness	Melancholy for the sister who remained in the institute

Table summarizes the writing of the diary by parents with respect to all the fields proposed by the format and to the indication provided. The "When" field reports the days when the parents filled out the diary. The "How" field considers the introduction of narrated episode, the description of the event occurred, and its consequences. The table also highlights the fields completed by parents. The "What" field present the "emotions" (experienced by each family member according to the writer's point of view; each emotion has a degree of intensity on a scale from 1 to 6) and the "events" (a brief summary of each event occurred).

Table 1.
Summary of the coding procedure of the case study.

confusion. Parents seem to show the discomfort created by the clash between expectations and reality, indicating their own ability to identify and express their emotions that the problems faced make them experience.

With regard to the girls (see **Figure 2**), only in some cases the emotions felt by them are listed. In more details, only one episode among those narrated during the journey (desperation referred to both girls) and four episodes (crossed, listed three times and referring only to one of the girls, sad referred to both of them) out of five narrated when being back to Italy were listed. The above mentioned data show an increasing attention to the moods expressed by the girls, above all in period after their arrival in Italy. It may be supposed that the need to organize a family routine leads parents to pay more attention to what is felt and experienced by the minors and above all to the most difficult events to manage.

Although only negative emotions were listed as felt by the girls, it seems advisable to analyze that information taking into consideration the number of episodes narrated compared to the time. Even in this case, it has to be underlined that the couple chose to narrate some specific episodes, thus not complying with the instructions given.

With reference to the intensity of the emotions, it is possible to observe that in the first episodes, a medium/high value is always listed, but from the sixth episode, no intensity is described. One of the hypotheses that can be made is that, over time, the level of intensity of the emotion expressed was regarded less essential than the identification of the same emotion.

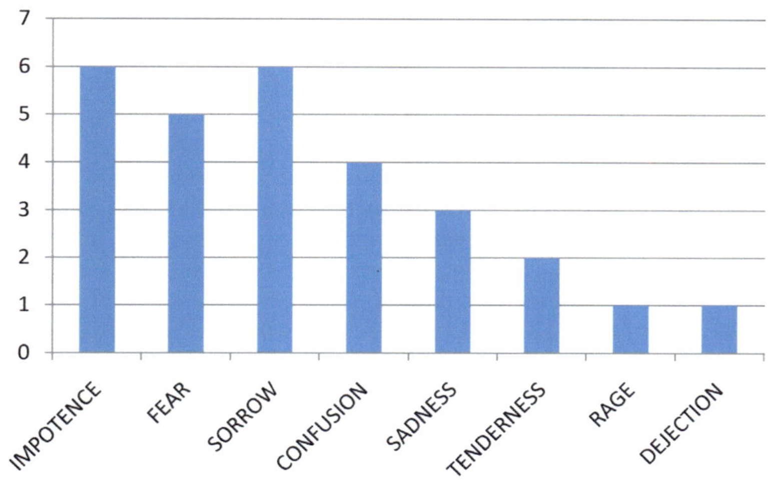

Figure 1.
The emotions described by the parents as felt by them. The results, represented in the graph, refer to the total number of times that parents have reported the emotion. Each emotion reported by the father or mother was considered.

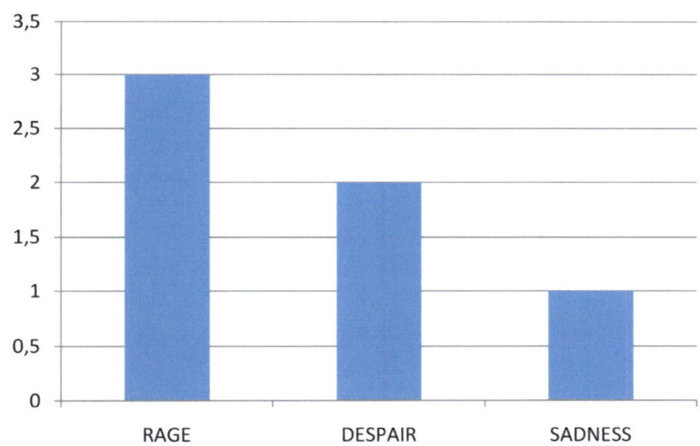

Figure 2.
The emotions listed by the parents as felt by girls. The results, represented in the graph, refer to the total number of reports about the emotions attributed by parents to the girls.

5.4 What: the events

The events narrated show some cohabitation issues and the solutions found by the couple.

The first is about the leaving of the orphanage, the most intense event on the emotional level, in which it is difficult to understand whether the tears of the girls are for what they are leaving, their poverty (they know they are leaving only bringing with them a small backpack containing just a few things), or for what they are going to face, and the adoptive parents obviously wonder if they themselves may be the cause of the girls' sadness.

Going on reading the episodes, regressive behaviors (thumb sucking, bedwetting, and incontinence during the day) referred to the oldest girl and the relevant worries of parents are described. The inconsistency between the behaviors adopted and the age of the girl causes reactions sometimes based on compassion, sometimes on reprehension. It could be useful to analyze those topics with the psychologist in charge of the case to look at the regression as an expected event and, at least in the beginning, beneficial as it is a sign of the need of the child to recover her own dimension of "being a little child in need of care."

Several references are made to the defiant behavior of the youngest sister over the first months of their life on Italy. It is interesting to observe the ability of the parents to recognize the emotion aroused by that behavior but also the opportunity described by them not to act out. Parents seem to express the need to keep up with the image of a loving, caring, patient, and sympathetic parent and had problems in managing negative and unexpected emotions.

The uneasiness of the girls to accept rules and frustrations is also described, but most evident is the feeling of helplessness parents experience when the girls show signs of homesickness and regret for what they left.

Therefore, parents describe moments of discouragement for which they try to give comfort or oppositional behaviors they try to contain: those actions shown ever appear to be poorly effective as they should be based on the certainty of a bond still being built. What is evident is the struggle of parents when trying to balance loving care with frustration as well as the ambivalence of the girls, who ask for attention but are scared by the new experience. The parents seem to manage a fragile balance between the desire to meet the requests of the children, which are ambivalent and cannot be met in a linear way, and the desire to reduce the riskiness of their bond, thus making the family life normal and reassuring the minors while reassuring themselves as parents.

The return to Italy and the placement in a new, larger family become the source of embarrassment due to some behaviors of the girls: grandparents are described as silent witnesses, observing what they think is due to the lack of educational skills of their own children.

5.5 The DAVAd in the relation between the clinician and parents

The above mentioned considerations, which are the result of the reading of the DAVAd, allow the psychologist who works with the couple to understand the dimensions of fragility that were emphasized by the meeting between the parents and the girls. Some of those considerations were introduced in the dialogue the psychologist had with the couple, during the first assessment session.

As provided for by the procedure detailed in the agreements between the country of birth of the children and the agency for international adoption, after the first months of cohabitation, a first assessment session of the adoptive family is held, following an interview structure suggested by the country of birth of the minors. In one section of the interview that has to be filled up, it is asked to analyze the level of adjustment of the girls and integration within the new family. Talking about those topics allowed the psychologist to recollect what parents had reported during the journey, reflecting on the meaning given to the events described and the impact they had on the parental couple. The couple seemed to be very aware of what they felt and experienced and was ready to regard it as elements of the dialogue. In this way, it was possible to talk about their need to be "a good parent," acknowledging the possibility that they may feel upset due to defiant behaviors. Furthermore, it was possible to reflect on the respect of the time of adjustment of their daughters, on the acceptance of "upsetting behaviors" by the girls on different occasions, and on their sorrow for the unease of the daughters that they cannot explain. Sharing with the parents the events occurred allowed the psychologist to help them to relieve their tensions, their feeling of being helpless, and their feeling of losing control over the experience made.

Furthermore, reading again the narratives of the DAVAd and noticing that mainly "negative and critical" events were narrated drove the "newborn parents" to also tell about the occurrence of many pleasant events and their joy to recognize themselves as a family. A more flexible narrative was therefore created, with the opportunity to acknowledge themselves as resilient and caring people.

In this research, it was useful to recognize and accept the experience of distrust and fear of the couple and at the same time the feelings of anxiety and fear expressed by the girls. The relation with the counsellor, who recognizes and legitimates what is felt and experienced by the parents without judging them, seems to have activated the resources of the couple useful to accept and legitimate the problems experienced by the minors.

6. Conclusions

A new tool was presented in this work, a narrative diary, which is the result of the considerations implicitly made reviewing the literature about adoption breakdowns. According to the literature reviewed, there seem to be two elements that may be useful to develop: the relationship between families and counsellors, as to launch early and long-lasting support services, and the attention to the "birth stage" of the family relations.

Therefore, a tool was designed that could be useful to guide adoptive couples and the counsellors working with them when monitoring of what happens during the stage of face-to-face contact with the children. A meeting in case of international adoptions takes place in the country of birth of the children and is difficult to be directly observed.

The act of writing a diary by the adoptive parents can thus make it easier to monitor a stage that is very important as it lays down the foundations on which the family relationship will be based. In addition to the monitoring of the first stages of the relations, such a tool is also not very intrusive and is meant not to harm the intimacy of the family being built.

The reading of the diary, on the other side, can provide counsellors with useful information to implement early actions of prevention aimed at safeguarding the wellbeing and development of the adoptive family, taking into consideration the way in which parents talk about their relationship with the children.

In more general terms, it can be stated that the act of writing is a preventive action, as it allows the actors to narrate about themselves and think back to the events that occurred.

According to Paradiso [51], narrative is the space for resilience, because narrating oneself and sharing one's own life experience with a "fairly good" interlocutor allow oneself to rethink the representation of the self and of one's own future. This is important for the adoptive couple in their relation with the counsellor, within a narrative path already started in the pre-adoption stage. And it is even more important for adopted children in their relation with the new parents, because they bring with themselves traumatic memories and are working hard at reconstructing their own story.

Even though the design of a tool is a small thing, compared to the desirable change in the culture driving the behavior of those who are involved in adoption processes, based on the evidence of our research, the diary proposed may be considered one of the elements that may drive such a change. It is a good pretext to help the ability of the spouses to think [52] of the family relationship and what happens within it every day, progressively walking away from a predictable interpretation of the events, based on habits according to which events are interpreted. Thinking about one's own emotiveness, aroused by complex relations, can be useful to any family, but it becomes highly significant for those families who since the beginning show relationship issues with their own children.

Author details

Barbara Cordella[1*], Paola Elia[2], Marzia Pibiri[1] and Alessia Carleschi[1]

1 Department of Dynamic and Clinical Psychology, Sapienza University, Rome, Italy

2 Society of Interpersonal Psychoanalysis and Analysis Group, (S.P.I.G.A.), Rome, Italy

*Address all correspondence to: barbara.cordella@uniroma1.it

References

[1] Bandini G. Narrazione e autobiografia nella famiglia adottiva. Rivista italiana di educazione familiare. 2008;**1**:110-119

[2] Hussey DL, Falletta L, Eng A. Risk factors for mental health diagnoses among children adopted from the public child welfare system. Children and Youth Services Review. 2012;**34**(10):2072-2080. DOI: 10.1016/j.childyouth.2012.06.015

[3] Lebrault M, André-Trévennec G. Adoption internazionale accompagnée. Devenir des enfants adoptés à l'international de 2001 à 2005 par l'intermédiaire de l'OAA Médecinsdu Monde. Neuropsychiatrie de l'Enfance et de l'Adolescence. 2015;**63**(3):141-156. DOI: 10.1016/j.neurenf.2015.01.008

[4] Wuyts R, Duret I, Delvenne V. Adolescentsadoptés: Un risque psychopathologique? Neuropsychiatrie de l'Enfance et de l'Adolescence. 2015;**63**(6):385-391. DOI: 10.1016/j.neurenf.2015.04.006

[5] Barone L, Lionetti F. Attachment and emotional understanding: A study on late adopted pre schoolers and their parents. Child: Care, Health and Development. 2011;**38**(5):690-696. DOI: 10.1111/j.1365-2214.2011.01296.x

[6] Burke RV, Prevention Group Research Team, Schlueter C, Vandercoy J, Authier KJ. Post-adoption services for families at risk of dissolution: A case study describing two families' experiences. Clinical Case Studies. 2015;**14**(4):291-306. DOI: 10.1177/1534650114556696

[7] Hartinger-Saunders RM, Trouteaud A, Matos Johnson J. The effects of post adoption service need and use on child and adoptive parent outcomes. Journal of Social Service Research. 2015;**41**(1):75-92. DOI: 10.1080/10926755.2014.895469

[8] Van IJzendoorn MH, Juffer F. The Emanuel miller memorial lecture 2006: Adoption as intervention. Meta-analytic evidence for massive catch-up and plasticity in physical, socio-emotional, and cognitive development. Journal of Child Psychology and Psychiatry. 2006;**47**(12):1228-1245. DOI: 10.1111/j.1469-7610.2006.01675.x

[9] Vadilonga F. Curare l'adozione. Raffaello Cortina: Milano; 2010

[10] De Bono I. Incontrarsi altrove. Il gruppo nell'adozione. Funzione Gamma. 2013. rivista scientifica telematica Sapienza Università di Roma; Disponibile presso: www.funzionegamma.it [Ultimo accesso 15 Ottobre 2018]

[11] Stovall KC, Dozier M. Infants in foster care: An attachment theory perspective. Adoption Quarterly. 1998;**2**:55-88. DOI: 10.1300/j145v02n01_05

[12] Paniagua C, Jiménez-Morago JM, Palacios J. Adopcionesrotas en Andalucía: Caracterización y propuestas para la intervención. Apuntes de Psicología. 2016;**34**(2-3):301-309. DOI: 10.22201/iisue.24486167e.2016.152.57612

[13] Ricerca italiana del 2003 commissione per le adozioni internazionali. CAI

[14] Semanchin-Jones A. Adoption disruptions and dissolutions [thesis]. St. Paul: Center for Advanced Studies in Child Welfare, University of Minnesota; 2010

[15] Rosnati R. La 'nascita' di una famiglia adottiva: sviluppo psicosociale dei bambini e benessere genitoriale.

In: Convegno Internazionale Allargare lo spazio familiare: essere figli nell'adozione e nell'affido; 13-14 febbraio 2015; Milano

[16] Coakley JF, Berrick JD. Research review: In a rush to permanency: Preventing adoption disruption. Child & Family Social Work. 2008;**13**(1):101-112. DOI: 10.1111/j.1365-2206.2006.00468.x

[17] CAI. L'accoglienza di bambini in stato di abbandono nel mondo: strumenti giuridici a confronto. In: Convegno sulla sostenibilità del Sistema adozioni internazionali della CAI e Istituto degli Innocenti; 19 ottobre 2018; Firenze

[18] Zuccalà MA. Rilievi giuridici e comparatistici del fallimento adottivo. Percorsi problematici dell'adozione internazionale. Commissione per le adozioni internazionali. Firenze: Istituto degli Innocenti di Firenze; 2003

[19] Vitolo M. Le difficoltà legate alla costruzione di un rapporto di affidabilità con la nuova famiglia: le storie e la memoria. Percorsi problematici dell'adozione internazionale. Commissione per le adozioni internazionali. Firenze: Istituto Degli Innocenti di Firenze; 2003

[20] Lombardi R. La famiglia adottiva al "banco di prova" dell'adolescenza, specchio che amplifica e confonde. Percorsi problematici dell'adozione internazionale. Commissione per le adozioni internazionali. Firenze: Istituto degli Innocenti di Firenze; 2003

[21] Luzzatto L. Il ruolo dei servizi. Percorsi problematici dell'adozione internazionale. Commissione per le adozioni internazionali. Firenze: Istituto Degli Innocenti di Firenze; 2003

[22] Bramanti D, Rosnati R. Il patto adottivo. L'adozione internazionale di fronte alla sfida dell'adolescenza. Milano: Franco Angeli; 1998

[23] Salvatore S. L'intervento clinico. Roma: Giorgio Firera Editore; 2015

[24] Zaccagnino M. I disagi della maternità. Individuazione, prevenzione e trattamento. Milano: Franco Angeli; 2009

[25] Ammaniti M, Tambelli R, Odorisio F. Intervista clinica per lo studio delle rappresentazioni paterne in gravidanza: IRPAG. Età evolutiva. 2006;**85**:34-44

[26] St-André M, Keren M. Clinical challenges of adoption: Views from Montreal and Tel Aviv. Infant Mental Health Journal. 2011;**32**(6):694-706. DOI: 10.1002/imhj.20329

[27] Ammaniti M, Gallese V. La nascita dell'intersoggettività. Lo sviluppo del sé tra psicodinamica e neurobiologia. Raffaello Cortina: Milano; 2014

[28] Paradiso L. Prepararsi all'adozione. Milano: Unicopli; 1999

[29] Harf A, Skandrani S, Radjack R, Sibeoni J, Moro MR, Revah-Levy A. First parent-child meetings in international adoptions: A qualitative study. PLoS One. 2013;**8**(9):e75300. DOI: 10.1371/journal.pone.0075300

[30] Guivarch J, Krouch T, Lecamus S, Vedie C. La filiation adoptive à l'épreuve du traumatisme. Annales Médico-Psychologiques. 2017;**175**(8):705-709. DOI: 10.1016/j.amp.2017.02.013

[31] Paradiso L. Stress post adozione e depressione post-adottiva: una distinzione importante [Internet]. 2007. Available from: https.//adozione percorsi.it/prospettive-psicologiche/stress post-adottivo

[32] Bolger N, Davis A. Rafaeli diary methods: Capturing life as it is lived. Annual Review of Psychology.

2003;**54**:579-616. DOI: 10.1146/annurev.psych.54.101601.145030

[33] Gunthert KC, Wenze SJ. Daily diary methods. In: Mehl MR, Conner TS, editors. Handbook of Research Methods for Studying Daily Life. New York, NY, US: The Guilford Press; 2012. pp. 144-159

[34] Lischetzke T. Daily diary methodology. In: Michalos AC, editor. Encyclopedia of Quality of Life and Well-Being Research. Dordrecht, Netherlands: Springer; 2014. pp. 1413-1419

[35] Sarmiento L, Skandrani S, Benoit L, Harf A, Moro MR. The experience of late international adoptees: A qualitative study. La Psychiatrie de l'Enfant. 2017;**60**(1):49-70. DOI: 10.1016/j.amp.2017.02.013

[36] Demetrio D. Scrivere l'adozione: Resilienza e passaggi di vita. Minori giustizia. 2011;**2**:31-40

[37] Freud S. Il poeta e la fantasia. OSF. Volume 5. Torino: Bollati Boringhieri; 1907

[38] Bion W. Transformations. London: William Heinemann Medical Books. Trad. it. Trasformazioni. Il passaggio dall'apprendimento alla crescita. Roma: Armando; 1973

[39] Matte Blanco I. L'inconscio come insiemi infiniti. Saggio sulla bi-logica. Torino: Giulio Einaudi; 1975

[40] Bucci W. Psychoanalysis and Cognitive Science. A Multiple Code Theory. New York: Guilford Press; Trad. it. Psicoanalisi e scienza cognitive. Roma: Fioriti; 1997

[41] Bruner J. The narrative construction of reality. Critical Inquiry. 1991;**18**(1):1-21

[42] Montesarchio G, Venuleo C. Narrazione generativa. In: Montesarchio G, Venuleo C. (a cura di). Colloquio Magistrale. La narrazione generativa. Milano: Franco Angeli; 2009. p. 71-105

[43] Pennebaker JW, Seagal JD. Forming a story: The health benefits of narrative. Journal of Clinical Psychology. 1999;**55**(10):1243-1254. DOI: 10.1002/(sici)1097-4679(199910)55:10%3C1243:aid-jclp6%3E3.0.co;2-n

[44] Solano L. Scrivere per pensare. La trascrizione dell'esperienza tra promozione della salute e ricerca. Roma: Franco Angeli; 2007

[45] Braga P, Tosi P. L'osservazione. In: Mantovani S, editor. (a Cura di). La ricerca sul campo in educazione. I metodi qualitativi. Milano: Mondadori. 1995

[46] Fonagy P, Target M. Attachment and reflective function: Their role in self-organization. Developement Psychopathology. 1997;(4):679-700. DOI: 10.1017/s0954579497001399

[47] Baldoni F. Alle origini del trauma: Confusione delle lingue e fallimento della funzione riflessiva. In: Crocetti G, Zarri A, editors. (a cura di). Gli dei della notte sulle sorgenti della vita, il trauma precoce dalla coppia madre al bambino. Pendragon: Bologna. p. 2008

[48] Bastianoni P. Funzioni di cura e genitorialità. Rivista Italiana di Educazione Familiare. 2009;**1**:37-53. DOI: 10.13128/RIEF-3332

[49] Slade A. Relazione genitoriale e funzione riflessiva. Teoria, clinica e intervento sociale. A cura di Zavattini GC. Roma: Astrolabio Ubaldini; 2010

[50] Chafe W. Some things that narratives tell us about the mind. In: Narrative Thought and Narrative Language. Hillsdale (NJ): Lawrence Erlbaum; 1990. pp. 79-98

[51] Paradiso L. Memorie familiari e narrazioni nella genitorialità e filialità adottiva. Rivista Italiana di Educazione Familiare. 2017;**1**:77-95. DOI: 10.13128/RIEF-20974

[52] Carli R, Paniccia RM. Analisi della domanda. Teoria e tecnica dell'intervento in psicologia clinica. Il Mulino: Bologna; 2004

Chapter 5

KidsTime Workshops: Strengthening Resilience of Children of Parents with a Mental Illness

Klaus Henner Spierling, Kirsty Tahta-Wraith, Helena Kulikowska and Dympna Cunnane

Abstract

This chapter will introduce children of parents with mental illness (COPMI) as a group and explain the impact and risk factors of parental mental illness on children. We will provide examples of approaches that can help children in this situation, using the KidsTime Workshop model as a case study. We will describe the approaches and methods of the KidsTime practice model and explain how a combination of family therapy and systemic therapy influences, together with drama, can create an effective multi-family therapy intervention. It will describe the impact of the KidsTime model, including testimonials from children and families, and highlight the evidence in support of preventative approaches, as well as the barriers to securing investment for these interventions. The chapter will conclude with recommendations for practice.

Keywords: parental mental illness, children, multi-family, systemic therapy, drama

1. Introduction

Children of parents with a mental illness face childhoods that can be full of challenging experiences, threatening their quality of life, development and long-term outcomes [1–4]. However, these children are not an officially recognised group in the UK, and data and statistics are not gathered about them. While UK policies recognise the needs of young carers, they do not address the specific challenges experienced by children whose parents have a mental illness. This is not the case in other countries; in Australia, these children are officially known as children of parents with mental illness (COPMI) and as "young relatives" in most Nordic countries. Children of parents with a mental illness remain a hidden group in the UK, and many are reluctant to identify as young carers due to the shame and stigma often associated with mental illness, making them vulnerable and at risk of neglect.

The UK Children's Commissioner Vulnerability Report (2018) found that in an average classroom, eight children have a parent with mental health problems—this is the equivalent to 25% of the UK school population [3]. In 2018, Our Time, a UK charity that advocates for and offers support to this group did an analysis of the existing data (supported by a team from Ernst and Young), which found that in excess of 3.4 million children and young people in the UK are currently living with a parent with a mental illness [5]. Further evidence indicates that, without support, 70% of these children are likely to go on to develop mental health problems themselves. With two ill parents, there is a 30–50% chance of the child developing a *serious* mental illness later in life [6]. A WHO review stated: "Children with a parent who has a mental illness or substance use disorder are placed at high risk of experiencing family discord and psychiatric problems. The intergenerational transfer of mental disorder is the result of interactions between genetic, biological and social risk factors occurring as early as pregnancy and infancy" [7, 8].

In Germany, where Our Time's partners, the "KidsTime Netzwerk", use the KidsTime Workshop model to support children and families, research has identified 3.8 million children affected by parental mental illness [9].

1.1 Summary of key facts and statistics

- In excess of 3 million children in the UK live with a parent with a mental health issue.
- Average of 8 children in an average classroom will be in this situation.
- 20–25% of the school population.
- 70% likely to develop a mental health condition.
- Parental mental illness is one of the 10 adverse childhood experiences (ACEs), which has a lifetime impact on both physical and mental health.
- Parental mental illness (PMI) is a root cause of many other ACEs.
- WHO identifies PMI as one of the most important public health issues of our generation.
- Intervention late after the onset of an ACE is less likely to be effective. Rising thresholds for acute support are exacerbated by significant reductions in early intervention spending by local authorities.
- By focusing on clinically diagnosable mental illnesses, the children and adolescent service (CAMHS) interventions are too late to address ACEs.
- In 2018 the Children's Commissioner reported that despite the new provisions in law, 4 in 5 young carers were not identified.

Research into adverse childhood experiences, known as ACEs [10], identifies parental mental illness as one of the ten most powerful sources of toxic stress in young people. The presence of mental illness in a parent is known to negatively impact a child's cognitive and language development, educational achievement and social, emotional and behavioural development [2–4, 10]. It can lead to anxiety and guilt coming from a sense of personal responsibility. Where there is severe mental illness in a parent and no second parent who is well it can lead to neglect or abuse. These children are also at greater risk of bullying, a lower standard of living and financial hardship [2–5, 9].

Figures 1 and **2** show the lifetime impact of adverse childhood experiences affecting the mental and physical health of the individual as a result of toxic stress.

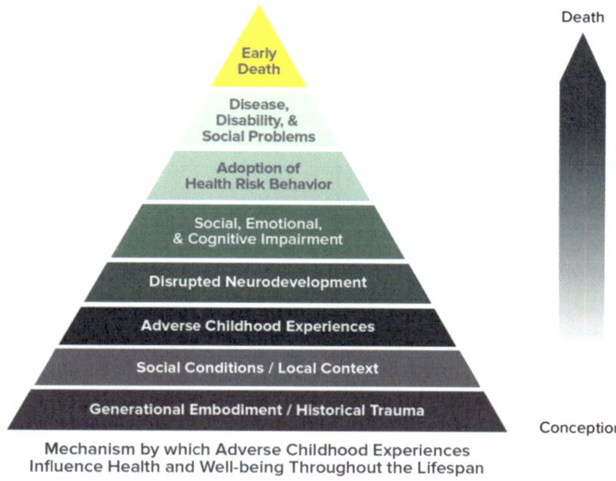

Figure 1.
The ACE pyramid (Centers for Disease Control and Prevention, cdc.gov).

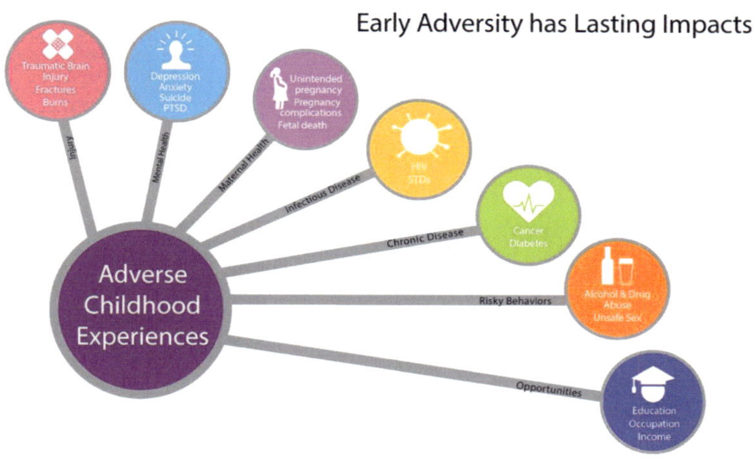

Figure 2.
Long-term effects of ACEs (Centers for Disease Control and Prevention, cdc.gov).

1.2 A hidden risk

The hidden status of these young people in the UK means that they have no statutory entitlement to specific support related to parental mental illness. Provision of formal, organised support or targeted intervention is therefore at the discretion of local funding bodies or entirely dependent on the voluntary sector. Any informal support is dependent on the awareness and understanding of professionals coming into contact with these children to identify and support their needs. However, this sometimes requires stepping outside of the remit of current practice and expertise, adding an additional "burden" to already high workloads. Additionally, many professionals report worrying about talking to children in this situation, as they are concerned about "*saying the wrong thing*" or "*making the situation worse*". Social service providers are dominated by risk concerns and are therefore reluctant to intervene in this area, which means that low intensity, early help is not commissioned. Despite these challenges, there are things that can be done to help children in this situation, enabling them to thrive, despite their adversity. There is evidence to suggest that relatively simple and low-cost interventions can build protective factors and the resilience of children and young people affected by parental mental illness, reducing their risk of harm and of developing problems themselves in later life [2, 11].

This chapter will explain the impact of parental mental illness on children and the associated risk factors. We will provide examples of approaches proven to help children in this situation, using the KidsTime model as a case study. We will describe the approaches and methods of this practice model and explain how a combination of family therapy and systemic therapy approaches, together with drama, can create an effective multi-family therapy intervention. We will provide evidence of the impact of the KidsTime model and highlight some of the barriers to securing investment for preventative approaches. The chapter will conclude with recommendations for practice.

2. Parental mental illness (PMI) and its impact on children and young people

This section outlines some of the common difficulties experienced by children and young people who have a parent with a mental illness. These include but are not limited to:

2.1 Parental emotional availability and its impact on the child-parent relationship

Research, using case studies and personal testimonies, depict the kinds of difficulties experienced by children and young people growing up in a family where there is a parent with a mental illness. For example, it is common for children, particularly younger children, to report experiencing the same symptoms as their parents, i.e., symptoms caused by the parent's diagnosis, such as delusions [12]. explains this can be due to the parent's illness limiting their emotional availability to their child. Both symptoms of the illness and side-effects of the medication can result in emotional withdrawal from the child, which the child typically perceives as rejection. The child therefore intensifies his or her attempts to achieve closeness with the parent, which may cause the parent to withdraw further. Not only does this create a vicious cycle of interaction between the parent and the child, but these attempts can expose the child to further risk, such as the distress of being drawn into the parent's psychopathological symptoms that are not their own. This is particularly likely in the absence of a sufficient explanation of the parent's mental illness that could enable the child to differentiate between behaviours caused by the illness and those that are not [12, 13].

2.2 Burden of caring roles and responsibilities on young people

The experience of living with a parent who has a mental illness often means that the child or young person often adopts caring roles in their family, which are not age-appropriate. They may fill any gaps in their parent's role, which the parent is not consistently able to fill themselves due to their illness. This is the case both when the parent is markedly unwell and thus genuinely less able and also when the parent is able, but the child has become used to fulfilling this role or does so in anticipation of the parent's next period of illness. The young person may care for their parent and other family members practically, through assuming responsibility for structuring the daily life of the family, fulfilling siblings' needs or household tasks, but also emotionally, in that their mind is occupied by issues related to their parent's wellbeing [12, 13]. These children also experience frequent role reversal, as they help their parent manage symptoms of their mental illness, such as emotional distress or behavioural difficulties. This often leads to *parentification* and loss of focus on the child's needs by both the affected parent and the child themselves [9, 14].

The long-term impact of such experiences can be that children in this situation gradually form a view of the adults around them as having limited capabilities and therefore do not trust or expect adults to meet their needs. The responsibilities they believe they must fulfil themselves are a large burden for a young person to carry. These young people will often experience feelings of guilt in taking over the parent's role and inadequacy, while trying, and inevitably failing, to navigate such unrealistic responsibilities. This can also negatively impact their own self-esteem and sense of self-efficacy, and they may start to question their capabilities in other spheres of their life, which also has an adverse effect on their wellbeing. This combination of taking responsibility for others and worrying that they are not up to it is often carried into later life and causes hidden stress and sometimes prevents them from fulfilling their full potential [14, 15].

2.3 Shame and stigma

Children of parents with a mental illness and their families suffer from the shame and stigma surrounding mental illness in multiple ways [9, 14, 16]. It hinders communication about mental illness and emotions more generally within the family. It also hinders communication and the development of supportive bonds outside of the family, i.e., with extended family, community and other social networks. This leads to feelings of isolation and withdrawal from social interaction [9, 14]. As a result, many children of parents with a mental illness feel very different to their peers:

> *"Well, all of last week I wasn't in (school), because I was ill. I think, sometimes, my friends might think that I've been avoiding them, or bullies might think they have affected me so much that I'm not coming to school anymore." (Young boy, KidsTime Workshop)*

> *"So, it's nice to finally meet people that know how it feels, especially, like in school, barely anybody would have the same situation, but when I come to KidsTime, there's all these people around me that have similar situations to my family and me." (Teenage girl, KidsTime Workshop)*

Such shame, stigma and isolation, combined with children's imagination, means many of these children live with damaging fears and/or misconceptions about mental illness. For example, they fear they will "catch" their parent's illness, that they are predetermined to developing it themselves, or that they caused the illness or its symptoms [15, 16]. The shame, stigma, fear and isolation further decrease the likelihood that they will ask for help, advice or information that would reassure them and enable them to make sense of their situation and develop strategies for coping with it.

3. Protective factors

The KidsTime model is built on three principles in its work with children and families affected by parental mental illness and will be described in more detail in the next section [2, 11].

1. Having a good explanation

2. Having a trusted adult to talk to

3. Knowing you are not alone

3.1 The importance of a good explanation

Many children affected by parental mental illness report receiving little or no information or explanation about their parent's illness. Even at the point of hospitalisation, only ~1 in 3 young people receive any information about their parent's situation [17]. Not having an explanation or not understanding what is happening can be an unsettling experience in itself. However, young people who have been given an explanation often identify this as a key factor in helping them to cope with their situation. Receiving an explanation about their parent's mental illness could make a significant difference in helping affected children to feel more in control of their situation. It could also mitigate the impact or even prevent the development of frightening misconceptions about mental illness and the confusion and self-blame many young people feel about the origins of the illness and its symptoms. This would enable children to differentiate between their parent's "ill" and "non-ill" behaviours and thus also decrease the likelihood of adopting any of these behaviours themselves [13]. Having a good explanation is one of three protective factors identified by international research as key in building resilience for children whose parent/s have a mental illness.

There is a lack of specialist support for children affected by parental mental illness in the UK. These children may cross paths with multiple services, such as health services, children's social care, schools or professionals directly involved in their parent's psychiatric or social care. However, these professionals do not have the awareness or understanding of the unique experiences of children living with, or caring for, a parent with mental health issues and also often lack confidence in speaking to children about mental illness. The negative impact of this is twofold: Firstly, it reinforces these young people's disillusionment with adults as protective or supportive figures. Secondly, these young carers remain under the radar and are therefore unlikely to receive a satisfactory explanation or helpful support. However, the potential harm and many of the risks associated with having a parent with a mental illness can be addressed by training adults to provide good, child-friendly explanations and appropriate support, which increase the protective factors and develop the child's resilience, examples of which will be given in the following sections.

4. Specialist intervention: the KidsTime Workshops

Adverse childhood experiences (ACE) have recently become the focus of research and public discourse. However, despite its official recognition as an ACE, parental mental illness has been somewhat overlooked in this debate, and there is no recognition or provision for children affected by parental mental illness in England.

Our Time is a UK charity that was set up to advocate on behalf of this group through raising awareness of the issue and developing specific support through the KidsTime Workshop approach, which has been adopted across the UK, Germany and Spain. These are multi-family support groups that combine systemic family therapy approaches, drama and play to provide families with the three protective factors outlined above. There are currently 12 KidsTime Workshops operational in England, supporting up to 250 children and their families.

5. The KidsTime model

KidsTime Workshops take place once a month, after school, for ~2.5 h, and are run by a multidisciplinary team of at least three members of staff. The model requires the following critical staff members:

- Clinical Lead, with a clinical background working in mental health services (often a psychiatrist or clinical psychologist or family therapist)
- Drama Lead, who has experience in creative and drama-led group work with children
- Logistical Lead/Coordinator, responsible for managing referrals, engaging and supporting families to attend the workshop and logistics (venue, equipment, transportation, etc.)

5.1 Workshop structure

5.1.1 Seminar (adults and children together)

The group begins with all staff and families, (typically 6–10 families per workshop), coming together for a playful activity, followed by a seminar-style session that explores a single topic related to (parental) mental illness. The Clinical Lead facilitates this session using informal discussion and playful activities. Importantly, the particular topic will have been identified by the families themselves as something they want to discuss, for example, what to do in a crisis.

The KidsTime Workshops have developed a model for explaining mental illness to children. Explanations are provided by the Clinical Lead, which is relevant to the seminar topic (i.e., not at every workshop). The Clinical Lead will employ visual aids and clear, simple and child-friendly language to describe how the brain works and how it can become "overloaded" as well as other aspects of mental illness (e.g., side-effects of medication) without being a diagnosis specific. An example of this can be seen in the videos, "*What does it mean to have a parent with a mental illness?*" and, for younger children, "*Making sense of mental illness*", available on the Our Time website: www.ourtime.org.uk.

5.1.2 Group work (adults and children separate)

After the seminar, the families separate into two groups, one for adults and the other for children, which run in parallel for 1 h. The children's group is facilitated by the Drama Lead. It starts with group games to help the children relax and focus, followed by drama work during which the young people create, rehearse, perform, and film a dramatic scene. The drama content will often be related to the seminar topic, but it is important that the children are free to set and interpret the topic themselves. The drama allows the children and young people to address issues of interest or concern without having to expose their own personal situation, giving them a voice and a way to explore different perspectives and reactions to difficult family issues.

The adult group consists of the parents or carers (sometimes guardians, grandparents or close relatives), with or without a mental illness, and explores their experiences of being a parent with a mental illness or supporting the family in which this is the issue, sometimes using the seminar topic as a starting point. The discussion is facilitated by the Clinical Lead who ensures that the experiences and needs of the children are a central focus. The adult group provides an opportunity for parents to talk more openly about their own experience and the challenges of parenting with a mental illness in a non-judgemental environment and to receive support and encouragement from one another.

5.1.3 Community time and reflection (adults and children together)

The children, parents and staff reunite after their respective groups for 30–45 min. First, everyone takes a break and shares food together (traditionally pizza because the children like it and it is easy to prepare). Then, everyone watches the film of the young people's drama, which leads to a collective group discussion about what the drama communicates and what insights the children and young people have demonstrated in their dramatisation. The parents contribute to the discussion by sharing a summary of their group discussion and their own reflections from watching the drama.

While the KidsTime Workshop model draws on some therapeutic methods and techniques, KidsTime is not designed as a form of therapy, but it is therapeutic in its effects. The design aims to create a community where the families can safely share their experience and knowledge and are listened to and able to ask the questions they need to ask without fear of judgement or having solutions imposed on them. The aim is to provide information, support and some relief to the families through a social intervention, while children and their needs remain the focus. Cooklin et al. state that an explicitly therapeutic intervention directed at the children may lead to the child seriously misjudging their predicament and adding to the sense that they (the child) are the problem and encourage further mistrust in adults [16] because they are not taken seriously. Firstly, the offer of therapy to the child may be falsely perceived as confirmation that they, like their parents, are going to develop a mental illness. Secondly, as these children will often adopt responsibilities beyond their years, in nature and volume, there is a risk that the child or young person would conclude that they are somehow failing to solve the problem or feel dismissed and undermined, if treated as a passive recipient of therapy. Therefore, the approach of professionals should aspire to take the role of an understanding, friend/mentor or relative rather than the formal and inevitably hierarchical role in which a therapist may be perceived.

> *"KidsTime has helped myself and my son to learn about my mental health, together. There's a great understanding of how they can help us, how they can help myself, my child, and, also, it's a place that you are accepted to have mental health (problems) and it not be a stigma. For the first time you can openly talk about any of your issues and concerns." (Mother, KidsTime)*

> *"Because it's somewhere where you can go to be with somebody that you know understands how you feel, and they might have the same situation too, and they just cheer you up, so it's a great place to go. Sometimes your parents are on medication or there is something wrong, so this just is a place to come to to calm you down." (Young boy, KidsTime)*

6. Key approaches

This section outlines some of the key approaches employed by the KidsTime model to achieve the desired protective factors, particularly and uniquely, an age-appropriate explanation of mental illness, its treatments and impact.

6.1 Systemic influences

The model views and encourages families to appreciate the systemic contributors to experiences; that the experience of each individual in the family results from their relationships with other members of the family; and what their feelings and thoughts about these relationships are. Based on this, the individual forms their view of themselves and perceptions of others. Bringing the whole family together to think about their situation and find ways of managing their lives in the context of the illness is one of the innovative and most powerful aspects of the model.

The KidsTime model recognises and aims to counter the potentially damaging effect of parental mental illness on the quality of social interactions within the family and with the wider social environment and support networks (other families and services, etc.) including social care providers, teachers and even the school. It aims to do so through facilitating communication between family members, with the focus of helping them understand the role of each person and the impact of parental mental illness on them. The model aims to promote social ties and trust between family members, neighbours and the general social world within which the family is located.

In general, families develop different patterns of internal communication and sharing of experiences. In families affected by parental mental illness, there is often little or no communication about the mental illness, due to shame and stigma, and a lack of understanding about mental illness [15, 16]. KidsTime Workshops aim to combat this stigma and social withdrawal by encouraging families to speak more freely about mental illness and finding creative ways to make this easier. Adapted systemic therapy methods, such as sculpture work, are used to help families visualise relationships and patterns of communication; this facilitates mutual reflection and discussion in the group helping them to identify their current patterns and how to develop healthier ones [18].

> *"My daughter, she was very quiet. She would sit in her room all the time and now, because of KidsTime, we can have half an hour to 45 minutes family time, and ask, "How has your day been?" and we can get a nice polite answer (from her). If anything does affect her, she can open up and get it off her chest, and if we can help, we can help." (Father, KidsTime)*

While the effect of parental mental illness on the children is the overarching focus of the parent and children's groups within the KidsTime model, parents' reactions to the impact of their illness are also actively discussed and considered. This results in children communicating their experiences to, and receiving feedback from, their family and the wider group (and vice versa), leading to a multi-systemic perspective rather than one-direction linear communication. This also leads to group interactions in which everyone is considered on the same level and equally able to contribute to discussion, thereby recognising the young people's knowledge and experience and the roles they perform within family life.

Also consistent with systemic approaches, the KidsTime model puts special emphasis on recognising and promoting families' capabilities. Families are respected as autonomous, self-organising systems and capable experts in their own situation. Within this, particular efforts are made to appreciate the young people's knowledge and expertise in their parent's mental health. Indeed, young carers will often notice signs of crisis or decline in their parents far earlier than the parent themselves or professionals. However, for a number of reasons that can be very frustrating and damaging for the child, this expertise is often invalidated in their interactions with the adults around them. Children and young people express frustration that they are often the closest observer of the parent and have responsibilities beyond their years and yet are not consulted, listened to, and frequently talked over by professionals. This combination of shouldering adult responsibility and being treated as a child who has no information or insight is particularly difficult and leads to mistrust and resignation on the child's behalf, adding to the notion that they are on their own with the problem and that adults cannot be relied upon, which leads to hyper-independence. The KidsTime model aims to be realistic about the different family situations and challenges and to support and empower affected young people within their roles to develop appropriate coping strategies that will help them to understand and manage their own situation rather than "fixing" the problem for them and importantly knowing what to do in a time of crisis and developing a network of people to whom they can turn to for help when they notice that their parent's mental health is deteriorating. This means that awareness raising and the education of professionals is a key factor in supporting these children and young people.

6.2 Multi-family work

Multi-family work is based on systemic approaches; it aims to combine the benefits of single-family therapy with group therapy while still encouraging the agency of all individuals participating.

The coming together of families in similar situations has multiple benefits, particularly when the shared experiences are as stigmatised and hidden as those related to parental mental illness. It enables affected families to discuss mental health issues without one child, parent or family feeling exposed, judged or different. It is also crucial that facilitators do not single anyone out. The KidsTime Workshop model encourages openness and reflection, and, through conversations about mental illness and common experiences, it reduces the often-associated stigma and shame-induced isolation. Unlike in the outside world, at KidsTime, the individuals and families are no longer the odd ones out:

> *"Since we've been coming here for a year and a half they (the children) get to see other children with parents with mental health (problems), and there's other families in same situation, so they don't feel so alone, because, I think, before, they thought our family was really strange. They've seen other people the same as us."*
> *(Mother, KidsTime)*

Multi-family work, in this context, is intended to enable solidarity and a sense of community between families, a sense that "we are all in this together". The individual family is viewed as part of the wider system of multiple families—a system that all families contribute to and benefit from. The families build a social network and mutually support each other. One of the most powerful ways in which this happens is the socialising and exchanging of experiences, ideas and advice facilitated by the multi-family model. In the KidsTime Workshop, families use each other as resources. Sharing in a multi-family group means they learn from each other's experiences and perspectives and are empowered to make changes themselves. In this sense, the multi-family model is intended to contribute towards helping families to help themselves; it allows individual parents and children to hear both positive and corrective responses from other adults and children, which may be both more acceptable and meaningful than comments from professionals [16, 18].

Actively involving families in discussion of similar problems in other families strengthens the self-esteem and agency of all involved. When experiencing difficulties, people tend to develop rigid and narrow ways of problem solving but are still often able to offer useful ideas to others in similar situations. Drawing on the expertise and experiences of families in similar situations leads to families viewing themselves more positively, as more capable. This strengthens self-esteem and the family's sense of agency and for the adults, in particular, a sense of pride as capable parents. In turn, this may enable families to become more resourceful and creative in finding solutions for their own difficulties [18]. Thus, the group becomes more powerful than any single therapist.

6.3 Drama work

Methods of creative therapy and drama work are powerful tools in creating a playful attitude and a relaxed, light-hearted atmosphere. This facilitates young people to have fun and foster positive relationships with each other and their families. It is within this type of setting that the young people are able to relax and to engage with drama as a powerful, therapeutic tool in the ways outlined below. Children of parents with a mental illness are often highly anxious and stressed, and the drama and games, first and foremost, allow them to forget their worries and just have fun, to be a child and to be able to play like a child, free from the burden of looking out for their parents, because they are safe in the parent's group.

In the young people's group, playful exercises are combined with devising and acting out fictional scenes together. Designing the content of these dramas acts as a channel of free expression for fear, anger and anxiety or other difficult emotions that a young carer may struggle to access and express in daily life. The invention of fictional characters also means children can choose to play out different perspectives and new narratives—ideals of who they want to be. This encourages optimism and gives them a sense of control over their situation, thereby enhancing their self-esteem and trust in their ability to take action.

While the dramas do address parental mental illness, they often do so in an indirect or metaphorical way. They allow the children to differentiate from the illness, exploring it from a removed and outside perspective and not getting caught up in it. Indeed, the staff are careful not to lead the young people into sharing their specific experiences, as the drama work is intended to act as a helpful tool to enable young people to explore their experiences from a distance, to make up stories and create roles that focus on general aspects of mental illness and crisis.

The dramas tend to capture the everyday experiences of the children and, in a more or less explicit way, the impact of their parent's mental illness. The dramas are filmed and played back to parents and staff and therefore serve as an effective channel for young people to communicate their experiences and fears. Moreover, the themes and experiences depicted in the dramas are not owned by one person; they are devised, played out and therefore communicated, as a group; this feels safer and less threatening for the young people to express and for the adults to receive.

The dramas are also useful in communicating important messages and explanations of mental illness to young people. The KidsTime model emphasises that explanations should address and challenge presumptions and fears that young people have about mental illness, for example, that they might "catch the illness themselves", which the dramas frequently illustrate. In order to reduce rigid ideas and fears about mental illness in young people, the dramas should also present mental illness as a changeable process rather than as a fixed, constant entity. Including the subject of mental illness in dynamic dramas is particularly useful as it depicts mental illnesses through characters' experiences rather than through listing signs and symptoms of diagnostic criteria.

The drama work contributes to the aim of the workshops in creating a space where "kids can be kids". The drama is part of a predictable and secure structure within which children do not take the lead, do not have to feel responsible and are thus able to relax and play in their more age-appropriate roles. In this way, the drama work enables the team to strike the important balance between the serious and the playful. The overall aim of the workshops is to provide a relaxed environment within which young people can explore and recognise their own roles, and the challenges within these, and have this validated by others while remaining optimistic and hopeful for the future. At KidsTime, young people are encouraged to recognise their successes and strengths despite their difficult situation and to have fun while doing so, which is enabled by creating an environment where they can engage in more age-appropriate roles and activities. The ability to play is a fundamental aspect of psychological health and creativity, and this is built into the method. It is noticeable that when children first come into the workshop, the ability to join in and play is very low but grows quite quickly once they feel safe.

> *"It's good, because we get to play games, and parents get to go upstairs, and we get to stay downstairs and have some fun."*
>
> *"KidsTime is a good place to go because you get to play games, run about, have fun and have pizza."*
>
> *"KidsTime is a wonderful place to go and you can express your feelings."*
> *(Testimonies from young children, KidsTime)*

6.3.1 KidsTime participant (aged 17)

> *"People think depression is when you feel low and want to kill yourself. But there is so much more to it than that. My mum has schizoaffective disorder. That means she gets schizophrenia symptoms, such as hallucinations, and mood disorder symptoms, including mania and depression. She mixes up reality with imagination. She takes antidepressants and sleeping pills but there is often no way of knowing what state she is going to be in.*
>
> *My dad found out about KidsTime when he was looking for ways to help me. I already knew about my mum's illness, but it was good to know that there are people who, like me, have to remind their parents to shower and eat.*
>
> *People say mental illness is invisible, but you can usually tell by the look on someone's face or the way they are not keeping up with personal hygiene that they are unwell. Being a carer for my mum is not a bad thing, but it is a responsibility. I know that sometimes she does not want to talk she just wants me to sit with her. The annoying thing is that because I have lived with my mum, I can usually tell when other people are down as well. You start to feel guilty if the people around you are not happy, which is illogical, but I cannot help it. That is one of the things we have talked about at KidsTime—the burden of having that insight. My school and college mates do not understand that, but with my friends from KidsTime we can just jump straight into a deep conversation, and that means a lot to me."*

7. Impact and evaluation of the KidsTime Workshops

To date, several evaluations of the KidsTime Workshops have been carried out, using a variety of methodologies, the findings of which are summarised in the following paragraphs. As a general rule, individual feedback forms are completed by the adults and children after each workshop. A study of the German KidsTime Workshops found that [19]:

- 95% of families submitting evaluations stated they benefited from attending the workshops and wanted to continue attending.
- All family members stated they had learned something new about mental illness at the workshops and that the workshops helped them to talk about mental illness within and outside of their families.
- Watching and reflecting on the children's drama film, as well as the multi-family group format (particularly the feeling of solidarity among families) were viewed as helpful catalysts in enabling the open discussion of issues that may have been perceived as being too "shameful" to talk about outside of the group.

Similar themes were present in the children's feedback; however, the most important impact for children was the sense of freedom they experienced in being able to return some of the responsibility to adults they could trust and talk to and in connecting with adults in a more positive way, challenging their previous thoughts and feelings about adults and professionals coming into contact with them and their families. The feedback especially highlighted how children experienced KidsTime Workshops as a secure framework within which they could act more freely [19].

In England, an evaluation by the Anna Freud Centre for Children and Families found that the workshops increased understanding of mental illness, improved parent-child relationships, reduced feelings of fear, shame and isolation and boosted confidence in children and young people [2, 11]. Due to the nuances and the number of factors at play within the workshops, Our Time has found that case studies are a useful tool in understanding the impact of these interventions on children and families. An analysis of recent family case studies in England has identified the following key themes: Rise in confidence among children and young people, improved relationships within and outside of the family, making new friendships and increased knowledge and understanding of mental illness.

Findings from the different evaluations undertaken to date demonstrate that the strength of the workshops lies in their ability to facilitate communication and positive relationship building within and outside of the family, providing effective peer support for children and parents and, in tackling the shame, stigma and misconceptions surrounding mental illness, reducing feelings of fear and isolation and raising young people's confidence and self-esteem [2, 11, 19].

8. The case for investing in preventative approaches

A common barrier to setting up and maintaining a KidsTime Workshop is securing funding for a preventative model. The fundamental rationale for the workshops is to prevent young people from developing psychopathology themselves. However, funding for support for people who do not have a formal diagnosis is almost impossible to obtain within curative and risk-oriented medical systems, which are often the result of restrictive fiscal policies that will only allocate funding for critical interventions. However, what such policies and approaches fail to address is that, without appropriate universal, preventative support in place beneath thresholds for critical services, the demand for these services will continue to grow at an alarming rate, leading to significantly increased costs in the medium to long term.

In relation to children of parents with a mental illness, the stakes are high. An estimated 3.4 million children and young people in the UK live with a parent with a mental illness. Without help, 70% (3.1 million) of these children will go on to develop mental health problems themselves at huge expense to the public purse [6]. For example, if a quarter of these young people develop depression by 2021, the projected cost to the UK government could be up to £470 million [5]. This is the tip of the iceberg—depression is just one of many ill consequences likely to befall this group. Other potential long-term consequences include disrupted education, restricted peer relationships (due to carer role), financial hardship, potential separation from parents, stigma, future physical and mental health problems, greater risk of suicide, unemployment, marital problems and crime and violence [2–5, 10]. Consequently, without intervention, the long-term prospects are bleak, and the cost of doing nothing could amount to £17 billion per year in the UK alone [20]. In comparison, the cost of preventative approaches is relatively small. To give an example, in England, it costs ~£2000 per family, per year, to take part in a monthly KidsTime Workshop, while an initial assessment by Child and Adolescent Mental Health Services costs £700 per child, prior to any intervention taking place.

While the case for prevention is clear, support for early intervention requires a culture shift across the health, social care and education system, which can only be achieved through policy change and the allocation of appropriate funds to facilitate this at a more local level. This will have to include training and awareness raising for professionals who deal with children in the course of their work, including adult mental health professionals. For this reason, organisations such as Our Time are campaigning for government to count the numbers of children affected by parental mental illness and to invest in prevention to help break the cycle of intergenerational mental illness.

9. Conclusion and recommendations for practice

This chapter has provided an overview of the workings and impact of multi-family approaches in supporting families affected by parental mental illness, using the KidsTime Workshops as a case study example. It has described the benefits of a more informal and non-therapeutic, multi-family intervention in helping children and families to understand and communicate about mental illness. As well as highlighting the potential risks associated with having a parent with a mental illness, it has demonstrated the power of receiving a clear explanation in helping children to understand and cope with their situation. Access to a supportive and non-judgmental environment where families can share experiences and talk to others in the same situation has been identified as a key protective factor for children and their parents, as illustrated in the feedback and testimonials from families listed in this article. Recommendations for professionals and practitioners working with children and young people affected by parental mental illness are to:

- Notice these children, and recognise the role they play in caring for their parents.

- Recognise and acknowledge that they are experts in their family situation, with often very advanced knowledge and insight into their parent's illness and/or behaviours.

- Provide children with clear explanations of their parent's illness and what is happening to the parent and for the reasons behind decisions (e.g., when a parent is hospitalised).

- Recognise that these children may fear or reject traditional interventions. Ask children what would help and listen to what they have to say, so that any support offered does not undermine or further isolate the child or young person.

Those interested in trialling multi-family interventions for children affected by parental mental illness should pay attention to the following principles:

- Create a relaxed, safe and supportive environment that is welcoming for parents and children.

- Avoid imposing traditional hierarchical structures, i.e., of professional and patient, and, instead, encourage staff to adopt the role of a friendly helper to facilitate trust and communication within and outside of the family.

- Provide clear age-appropriate explanations for mental illness.

- Use a range of creative methods, such as drama, to engage and make it a fun experience for children, to enable exploration of the subject from different perspectives and to encourage reflection.

Further information and guidance about the KidsTime model, including how to set up a KidsTime Workshop, is available on the Our Time website: www.ourtime.org.uk.

Author details

Klaus Henner Spierling[1*], Kirsty Tahta-Wraith[2], Helena Kulikowska[2] and Dympna Cunnane[2]

1 Agaplesion Diakonieklinikum, Rotenburg, Germany

2 Our Time, London, England

*Address all correspondence to: h.spierling@diako-online.de

References

[1] Wiegand-Grefe S, Jeske J, Bullinger M, Plass A, Petermann F. Lebensqualität von Kindern psychisch kranker Eltern. Zusammenhänge zwischen Merkmalen elterlicher Erkrankung und gesundheitsbezogener Lebensqualität der Kinder aus Elternsicht. Z f Psychiatrie, Psychologie und Psychotherapie. 2010;**58**(4):315-322

[2] Cooklin A. Promoting children's resilience to parental mental illness: Engaging the child's thinking. Advances in Psychiatric Treatment. May 2013;**19**(3):229-240

[3] Children's Commissioner Vulnerability Report. 2018

[4] Welsh Adverse Childhood Experiences (ACE) study. Public Health Wales. Centre for Public Health, Liverpool John Moores University; 2015

[5] Ernst and Young. Sizing the Problem—Analysis. Our Time

[6] Rubovits PC. Project CHILD: An intervention programme for psychotic mothers and their children. 1996

[7] Effective Interventions and Policy Options, WHO (2004). Parents with Mental Disorders and Mental Health Fact Sheet 2016. Available from: www.who.int/mediacentre/factsheets.f220/en/

[8] Hetherington R, Baistow K, Katz I, Trowell J. The Welfare of Children with mentally ill parents: Learning from Inter-country comparisons WHO paper. 2001

[9] Mattejat F, Remschmidt H. Kinder psychisch kranker Eltern. Deutsches Ärzteblatt. 2008;**105**(23):413-418

[10] Felitti Vincent J, Robert A, et al. Relationship of childhood abuse and household dysfunction to many of the leading causes of death in adults. The adverse childhood experiences (ACE) study. American Journal of Preventative Medicine. 1998;**14**(4):245-258

[11] Evaluation Report of KidsTime Workshops, Anna Freud Centre, (2010-2011). KidsTime Workshop Manual, & Wolpert. An exploration of the experience of attending the KidsTime programme for children with parents with enduring 7 mental health issues: Parents' and young people's views, Clinical Child Psychology and Psychiatry; 2014

[12] Wiegand-Grefe S, Cronemeyer B, Plass A, Schulte-Markwort M, Petermann F. Psychische Auffälligkeiten von Kindern psychisch kranker Eltern im Perspektivenvergleich. Kindheit und Entwicklung. 2013;**22**(1):31-40

[13] Cooklin A, Cunnane D. Learning from the kidstime model. Rotenburg: Conference bag-kipe; 2018

[14] Wagenblass U. Risiko-und Schutzfaktoren bei Kindern psychisch kranker Eltern. In: Vortrag im Rahmen der Fachtagung vom Runden Tisch in Braunschweig: Frühe Kindheit—Frühe Hilfen; 2009. Im Web: https://wwwvhs-braunschweigde/vhshdf/downloads/hdf-fachtagung/Prof-Dr-Wagenblass_15-05-09pdf [Zugriff: 4 November 2015]

[15] Wiegand-Grefe S, Halverscheid S, Plass A. Kinder und ihre psychisch kranken Eltern. Familienorientierte Prävention—Der CHIMPs-Beratungsansatz. Göttingen: Hogrefe; 2011

[16] Cooklin A, Bishop P, Francis D, Fagin L, Asen E. The Kidstime Workshops. A Multi-Family Intervention for the Effects of Parental Mental Illness. London: CMHS Publications; 2012

[17] Bohus M, Schehr K, Berger-Sallawitz F, Novelli-Fischer U, Stieglitz R, Berger M. Kinder psychisch kranker Eltern. Eine Untersuchung zum Problembewußtsein im klinischen Alltag. Psychiatrische Praxis. 1998;**25**:134-138

[18] Asen E, Scholz M. Praxis der Multifamilientherapie. Heidelberg: Carl-Auer; 2012

[19] Spierling KH. Kidstime workshops—ein Projekt mit Multifamilienarbeit für Familien mit psychisch erkrankten Elternteilen. Systeme. 2016;**30**(1):54-74

[20] The Cost of Late Intervention: Early Intervention Foundation Analysis. 2016

Chapter 6

Mirage: Possibilities and Limitations of Experiencing Foster Home as a Family

Eva Mydlíková

Abstract

The theme of this chapter is the life of children living in state foster homes of the so-called family type. The theoretical scope of the research on the quality of life is based on the chosen capabilities according to the theory by Martha Nussbaum. The qualitative strategy has been chosen as a base for the methodology of the research. Predominantly, the deductive method has been used for collecting and processing the research data by openly coding the transcripts of clinic interviews with children living in foster homes. The research has been searching for answers to these four questions: How can children, living in foster homes, develop cognitively? How can children build relationships and emotions in foster homes? What does the term "home" mean for children living in foster homes? How do children living in foster homes perceive their own identity? Among the most important research findings belongs the information on an excessive burden of adoption on the children, on a weak engagement in creation and improvement of children's home, on wrong conditions for the self-development, self-evaluation and self-reflection of a child and other.

Keywords: capability, child, foster home, quality of life

1. Introduction

There are children living everywhere in the world, for which their parents cannot or will not care. Every society creates its own mechanisms to cope with this phenomenon. That applies to Slovakia with its over 5 million population as well, marked by the culture of central Europe, Christian values, but also by a half-century of the socialism regime. The socialistic period of the life of society has been defined by the state monopoly and by a high centralization of provided social help to citizens, which practically meant a high rate of the provided social care in the state residential form. That brought along the uniformity, poor range of forms provided, and a high rate of passivity in clients. After the 1989 revolution the passive approach of social care has changed into active approach of social help, which also applies on the area of help for children. Post-revolutionary legislation has broken down the state monopoly on providing the social services and socio-legal protection of children and offered participation to private subjects. The enforcement of social help has been decentralized into public and private providers. *The Agreement on rights of a child* and consecutively established *Directives of the United Nations on the foster-family care* have been an important influence on socio-political and economic change in the approach towards child care. The government of Slovak republic has elaborated the *Strategy of deinstitutionalization of the system of social services and foster-family care* and ever since 2011 creates legislative, social and economical conditions to support a life of children in their natural, foster and community environment. The state policy after the revolution prefers child care in a family in the form of foster personal care, step-family care and personal care of a legal guardian. According to the records of the divisions of socio-legal child protection there are approximately 2,24,000 families in Slovakia [1]. In 2016, 1,058,300 children have been living in Slovakia, out of that 14,065 children (1.33%) have been living without their own home. Based on the court order, 744 children have not managed to find their home by above stated forms, 1468 children have been placed into professional families, 835 children (17.60%) have been placed into other groups and 2441 children (51.45%) have been placed into individual groups in a foster home [2]. Namely the group of these 2441 children living in a foster home has been a subject of interest to the qualitative research of which the results are being presented in this thesis. The task of a foster home is to temporally provide an alternative natural family environment to a child or to create a replacement of the family environment. Through its executive branches, the state provides and ensures for children: housing, food, services, personal equipment of a child, safe keeping of precious things, health care, mandatory school attendance and preparation for career [3] and in this way the state tries for an integration and individual approach towards the child. The integration approach is used in a sense of closing the conditions for integrating child into local communities (professional families and groups properly arranged and localized under conditions on a level of community), as well as creating conditions for integrating children with less serious development disorders into professional families and individual groups. An individual approach is based on an application of professional methods, forms and programs for working with children that require a special approach [1]. The aim of this chapter is to describe research findings on life children living in a foster home of the so-called family tape considering the capability phenomenon.

2. The capability of children approach

The capability concept stems from the approach of "child's well-becoming." This approach, preferred more or less up to the 80s of the last century, perceives child as a little person who experiences the in-between state towards adulthood, ergo a future adult. This approach is focused on the future of the child. The central point of interest is to ensure that the child gets good education and has good health once the child reaches the adulthood and this should be predisposed by a proper parental care. However, these goals can be formed by an adult person only. All in the name of child's well-becoming. The child alone is perceived only as a passive receiver of these benefits [4, 5].

Decreasing birth rate, unsteadiness of human relationships in family and society, centralization and fixation of partnerships through child, have concluded into a need of a new legal position of a child, brought by the Agreement on rights of a child [6]. The situation of society in the postmodern period has brought an orientation of the society on the individualization of a person, built on the reflection [7]. This way, the "well-becoming" has changed the approach to "well-being." This approach considers children as active participants and carriers of rights. New priorities are asserted, for example, a much higher engagement of children in achieving social skills, their engagement as citizens, and their part in creating the culture of the society. The theoretical developments of the child's well-being approach have been built at first in the concept of life quality. The reason for this has mostly been the attempt at quantification and measurement of the extent of child's well-being, as the phenomenon of human happiness has been difficult to measure and it was too vague. Sociably acceptable indicators as well as methods for their reading and measuring have already existed in that period in the area of life quality. It was assumed that it would be mainly social indicators that could influence the children's life conditions [8–10].

In the 60s of the last century UNICEF has published a report on the state of children, in which it also published the results of measuring the life quality of children, as well as socio-demographic trends, risks and needs of children [5, 11–15]. In the 90s of the last century the Nobel Prize winner for economics, Amarthy Sen, has started to promote the so-called *capability approach* [16–18], further developed by the philosopher Martha Nussbaum [19–22]. Both had decided that the *capability* is an ability of an individual to achieve such a life the individual can value. Therefore, the *capability approach* is mostly about social arrangement of a just approach to such living conditions that the individual values himself. Both have understood that not every person has the same options of freedom and choice to reach a dignified life. They tried to find out what are the necessary expectations, options and skills people need to reach their goal. According to Nussbaum [22], in every society individuals exist who cannot even form their rights not to say fulfill them, therefore, they need support. In this classical understanding is the capability a connection: fulfilling individual's needs, human prosperity, material conditions, and fulfillment of individual needs, human desires and emotions. These characteristics have an interdisciplinary aspect of well-being. In this context, Robeyns [23] talks about the capabilities as substantive freedoms. Nussbaum [21] has formulated 10 basic capabilities; in 2014, Bigeri has presented 14 of them [5]. Martha Nussbaum described these following functions of human capabilities: (1) normal length of life—a person should not die prematurely; (2) good health—a person should have an option to enjoy good health, have appropriate care; (3) physical integrity—have the option of a free movement, a feeling of safety, protection of personal space); (4) utilization of senses, perception and thinking—access to information, education, space for self-expression, for searching for one's own meaning of life, religious freedom, freedom of expression; (5) emotions—option to create relationships with things and people, to love and to be loved, option to safely relive anger, love and other emotions; (6) practical thinking—option to create goodness, actively plan one's life, option to realize one's own plans; (7) relationships—option to live with others, participate in social interactions, empathy, to have self-worth and respect others, protection from discrimination, reciprocal appreciation; (8) other living creatures—to have the option to relive the relationship with animals, plants; (9) game—option to play, entertain and relax; (10) control over one's own environment—have the right to engage, associate and protect one's own work, as well as to own a property. At first glance, these 10 capabilities might sound a little bit generalized, stemming from the combination of some human rights and psychological, biological and social human needs. In spite of this overall universalism is out of it built a theoretical scope of quantitative research the subject of which was capability of children, living in foster homes in Slovakia in 2016–2017.

3. Research methods and realization

The content analysis has been used in the quality research, which was originally only quantitative research method [24]. However, the arrival of quality method of the research has influenced its usage in quality research as well [25, 26]. The aim of our research was to find out how can children living in foster home lead a life they would like to lead. Through 2016, we have realized 35 in depth interviews with four categories of participants: children between the age of 6 and 14, children above 15 years old, young adults and professional employees of three foster homes. Foster homes have been chosen for the research on the basis of two criteria: its capacity should top 70 children and they should have been from various regions. Children have entered foster home either from biological families or from professional, in some cases foster families. The selection of concrete children for the interview has been done on the basis of their age, sibling relationships and mainly proclaimed willingness of a child to talk. The bottom age line was stated by the legislation that in Slovak republic does not allow children below the age of 6 to live in a residential facility. The exception consists of children with grievous health disadvantage, living in specialized socio-health facilities who can be younger than 6 years. In this chapter we present the results of the group of children between the age of 6 and 14, living in individual nurture groups of family type. The nurture group of family type itself has its own budget that is usually around 6–10 children. The group consists of siblings, filled in by other children. The group is therefore heterogeneous in age and gender. Children should participate in domestic chores, they should learn individually how to manage finances: foster home is divided spatially into several units—stand-alone nurture groups and some of them can be in a family home outside of the main domicile of the foster home. Children share rooms in two or three, have a shared living room and kitchen. Six employees alternate fixedly, usually consisting of a team of educators, social and therapeutic educators, housekeepers. A psychologist and social worker is employed in the foster home as well. From 29 hour footage we have transcribed a 406 page long transcript. This transcript formed the research sample. For one unit of analysis were considered quotes of children, regarding the way of life in the foster home. We have acquired on one side manifest contents, obvious from interviews and latent contents on the other side, that result from verbal as well as non-verbal utterances of children during the interview, located in its in-depth structures. We have created four research questions: (1) How can children living in foster home develop cognitively? (2) How can children in foster home develop their relationships and emotions? (3) What does the term home means for children in foster home? (4) How children from foster home perceive their identity? (5) When analyzing the transcripts of the recorded interviews we used symbolic interactionism, which Hendl [27] considered to be the basis assumption of the correct application of the grounded theory approach and the modification of which [28–31] we used to process our results. Our goal was to clarify the phenomenon of the capability of children living under the conditions of an institution that simulates the family environment. The capability phenomenon is presumed in the context of strictly recorded data that anchor it into theoretical frameworks. The primary focus of this research is capability of children. Through a three-level coding (open coding, axial coding and selective coding), we have abstracted variables that lead to the formation of the conceptual scheme describing relationships between the obtained variables.

4. Process of analysis

We have collected the data through in-depth interview that we have record on the audio-record and transcribed into transcripts. The transcripts were coded at first, and then we have repeatedly checked their suitability considering the observed factors of children's capability. Some were discarded; some were modified and consecutively used in the next sequence of coding. In the research we have follow the rules of ethical research. A high probability of subjectivism in interpretation of collected data was minimized by having four researchers work at the same time. Even though each one had their "own" age group of participants, the strategy of acquiring and processing the data had been mutually agreed upon. We processed the transcripts of the recordings into a spreadsheet form [32], which allowed us to freely add text to the rows and columns into a final representation.

When naming the statements, we used the procedure of asking questions [28]. The child's statements have already been conceptualized in the first step. The goal of interviewing the child was to identify categories of its life experience (capabilities) in the context of possibilities and limitations provided by living in foster care. Even at this stage of open coding, we had an idea about these categories, but we tried to schematize them and interpret them as objectively as possible by using codes. Another level of coding, so-called axial coding, was used to construct the main categories into a concepts [28, 30, 33] and thus to try to find their properties and characteristics. The subcategories resulting from open and axial coding have been allocated into seven outcome categories of research findings. We have assigned them to the selected Nussbaum capabilities. We compared the outcomes to the descriptions of the selected capabilities in order to create a solid structure for interpreting the research data. At the outset, Nussbaum's capabilities have mainly been used to form a framework for creating the questions asked in the interview. At the end of the process, they were used again to form a framework that would keep us from straying from the validity of the research.

5. Outcomes

The outcomes obtained during this research were divided into four categories. These give an insight into the extent to which children in foster care can live the life they want for themselves.

For better clarity, we sorted the obtained results according to selected Nussbaum capabilities.

5.1 Capability 4

Use of senses, ideas and thoughts—access to information, education, space for self-realization, for searching one's own, meaning of life, religious freedom, freedom of expression **Tables 1** and **2**.

Recording of the interviews with children had started on the last day of the school year. The report and the school were therefore a spontaneous theme number one in our interviews. Children talked by themselves about not liking to attend school, about almost all of them having postponed the school attendance and at least half of them visits school with special needs. This quantification is not as interesting considering the low numbers of participants. However, interesting is the way of attendance in specialized schools. A child, after being taken out of a family, has been by the court order placed into a foster home—an institution of residential type. Considering the social deficits of the family, the child comes to the foster home and most probably with the postponed school attendance or with very bad school achievements, which is usually caused either by socially uneventful environment or by undiagnosed or deeply neglected learning disability. Almost automatically, child switches into a school for special needs. Considering the integration at Slovak schools is only a wish, child is moved into a school for children with special needs. These are almost all of the dormitory type; build in socialism regime on the edge regions with hard accessibility. Therefore, the child leaves on Monday the residency of foster home and enters the residency of specialized school, which the child leaves again on Friday afternoon, to come back to foster home. For example, even a 7-year old child must manage adaption in two residential systems!

Codes	Bad school results; problems with mathematics and English; deferred schooling; school for children with special needs; disinterest in learning; school with Slovak/Hungarian language; ADHD; expelled; likes to help the school janitor; indifferent towards/dislike of teaching staff; the closest classmates are from foster care; they live in special needs school for 5 days—that is not a home, they just sleep there—and spend the 2 holiday days in children's care home; should improve school results but; would like to become a chef, carpenter, but does not do anything to achieve this; I can help myself, but ... without hobbies, interests; art—I am very good at it (reality is different); I have a talent to draw, but I do not do extracurricular activities; next year I am going to finish the drawing and attend a competition; the size of the drawing matters; I enjoy IT technologies, computers (does not have any); I exercise and climb trees (never attempted to climb one), likes owls because they have beautiful big eyes; painting; likes to play football, but is better at ice hockey (never played it); likes to go out, get a soda, go swimming, but not with kids from foster care... Jumping, badminton, third place and he also wins at tennis (never played it); I like water (sister can swim)
Categories	Bad school results are associated to disinterest in learning; almost all children have deferred school attendance and are 2 years older than other children in their year; children in schools for special needs children have better results, but significant problems with adaptation; even though the children are integrated in classes, relationships with other classmates are limited to "foster kids"; an important role in the school environment is played by "service" persons in the school—a tutor, a janitor; unclear professional career, no goals; in calmer children, interest in drawing and playing on a computer; in more excitable children, interest in climbing, cycling, football, tennis, other physical activities; hobbies are monothematic and there is a lack of diversity; a high manifestation of individuality in this environment is the interest for owls, which is not further developed because of finances
Concepts	The disadvantaged starting position in school is unmotivating for children, which reflects in poor performance and then results in lack of education and the absence of a professional career development. Children, with limited cognitive capacities, must from an early age adapt to two systems at the same time: school and home. Children appear to be sharing a sort of leisure time activities model among themselves. Activities aim to ventilate the accumulated energy. It is in this area where one can observe the largest disproportion in self-reflection. Children present results that they neither really reached, nor even tried to confront. The only real results were achieved by a boy who was led to the activity by the professional foster parent (shooting sports)

Table 1.
Children and the development of cognitive skills.

Home preparation for classes is a group thing. As a daily program, children have classes when they study, during which the employees have their chores connected with the run of "household." Since the groups are heterogeneous by age, both first-years and high schoolers share the place and time for homework—disregarding whether the child is focused, motivated and whether the child understands the covered topic. It seems that children lack motivation the most. One can say that low school achievements and low social background practically push children into special groups of "outsiders" at school, which only strengthens the already bad social status and children circle in the identity of "fosters." Similar findings are presented by Milan Fico from the "Institute for Research of Labour and Family" [34], who in his extensive research from 2017 talks about "rare instances of supporting a child in meeting his or her individual needs."

Through the communication with children we have noticed very weak vocabulary of our participants. This is strongly constricted by a "lexicon" of foster surrounding and TV program. Children have problems to orient in time. A study of the "time perception" of children at foster homes would be considerable, because a child during the interview had his own "time anchors" which we as researchers did not understand much. Despite the fact that children reach the age of professional decision-making (14–15), no one works with them systematically on building their professional career. Children automatically accept the "traditions" of the foster

Codes	Trains 3× a week (only been once); cycling; shooting; I won a second place at world championships! Tomorrow I am going to camp—that is in 3 days; then we are going to be at dad's for 2 weeks and from Friday. We came to the children's care home, do not know, not sure, long time ago. At some point. I do not know how old I was, but I was 6 years old and I have been there for 8 years (is currently 10 years old); Fero murdered my brother, we washed up and were taken away in a car... I do not know how long I have been here. Was it snowy or was it summer? We did not go to school on Monday (holidays). I came here with Dominik—when?—When Tomas was in a different family. They had to leave house. When? Because grandfather was yelling at dad
Categories	The perception of the current time is relatively good, but the events of the past cannot be "anchored"—not even by significant holidays or by events
Concepts	The perception of time lacks continuity, children struggle to place events in time and do not understand the past. They lack understanding of what happened to them at home and therefore they are unable to explain their own role and involvement in any of this

Table 2.
Children and the development of cognitive skills-time.

home and attend the same high school as the foster children before them, not thinking about the major of the given high school not being in their point of interest. The foster home functions, in a way, as a sub-supplier of children for regional high schools. Similar findings are presented in the research on the life perspectives of young adults after the end of their stay in the foster care, authored by Juhásová [35]. The group approach is visible in the interests and hobbies of the child. If some child even shows interest in something outside of supported foster home activities, the child has no chance to develop his interest further. The reason for absence of an individual approach is the lack of employments, weak ability and missing tradition to organize volunteers, who would have time to spend with children individually, as well as deficit of financial means to pay the quality hobby groups.

5.2 Capability 5

Emotions are the ability to create bonds with things and people, to love and to be loved, the possibility of experiencing anger, love and other emotions and capabilities in a safe environment **Tables 3** and **4**.

5.3 Capability 6

Relationships are the opportunity to live with others, to participate in social interactions, ability to empathize, self-esteem and respect of others, protection against discrimination, mutual recognition (**Table 5**).

The second category of the research results consists of relationships and emotionality of children. Children come to the foster home usually on the basis of an incident in the family, where the trigger is usually the process of taking the child away from the family. Thus, usually all the children living in the particular family enter the foster home at the same time. These children have common family history, therefore having sibling identity as well. If nothing changes in the way of life of parents, the incident repeats itself again after several years, now with different, younger children in the family. These children enter the foster home and meet their siblings living in the foster home for years. The sibling relations of these two sub-categories are only biological. Moreover, older children have the feeling that the younger ones were "enjoying" their parents, while they were "stuck" in the foster home. Among the siblings is then strong, almost hateful relationship. If the parent switches partners too often, the connection of these siblings is only their

Codes	Visits father every day—he has 16 children—he lives with one of them; they know their parents but they hate them; parents tortured him; his life is great without the parents; father would not take me because he cannot afford to pay for my schooling and foster care will provide education for me; hates his mother; likes her mother; mother has a boyfriend; they are expecting a new child together; father is in prison; parents do short visits of their children in foster care; they always take the kids for walks one by one; children are jealous of each other; regressive desires to be cuddled up in one's arms; parents always promise and children blindly believe; parents treat children differently and take each of them home for different periods of time; brother lives in a different children care home; grandmother used to visit, she died, now no one visits; grandmother visits with grandfather, and auntie too; they cannot go to their parents', they live somewhere else now, they do not have money, they have other kids, they do not have a mobile phone...
Categories	There is a more regular and intense contact with one parent; the other parent is ignored, perceived as the weaker one, there are tendencies to always find excuses for them; children get constant disappointments from their parents' promises; if they are less in contact with the mother, they despise her more than they would the father if it was the other way around; in case of family violence, there is a categorical rejection of any connection the parents; grandparents and other relatives create emotional backing for the children; parents take siblings home, or for walks, individually one by one making children jealous of each other
Concepts	Children without a contact with their parents are appreciative of their life in the children's care home; if children have an occasional contact with one of the parents, they have regressive desires towards them

Table 3.
Children and the emotional development—parents.

Codes	Telephone contact with godmother, with uncle; siblings usually stick together in pairs if they got to the foster home together; as if they did not have a capacity for more than a coalition of two; outside of the coalition if they are step-siblings, but they were problematic together, which is why they had to leave the family; she likes her sister because they play together; brother beats them; they do not know where are the other siblings, but they do not care; they know the names of specific employees of the children's care home when they like them; when I am said I go to my sister, brother (from the coalition of two), miss (care worker), I hide in my bed alone and I cry; Mum's boyfriend stabbed her with a knife, and brother as well... I was afraid; they took us away
Categories	Siblings divide themselves into real- and step-siblings; children pair up in sibling coalitions of two and are actively aggressive towards third, and other; the child outside this coalition is perceived as problematic, the one who is responsible for their punishment; at a time of emotional crisis, children seek closeness of the sibling from their coalition, occasionally a care worker, but they are often alone; no one is then helping the children to process heavily traumatic events
Concepts	As if the children did not have a potential to be close to more than one sibling The strongest coalitions form with children who came to foster care together—they have a common crisis history that leads to a stronger mutual bond The sibling who is "outside" this coalition is actively and passionately hurting the coalition of two with No one is helping the children to process the traumatic events witnessed and experienced by them (the murder of smaller brother, attempted murder of mother and older brother) Children do not know the reasons why they had to leave their own families, or even foster families, and thus they are creating incorrect cognitive schemes

Table 4.
Children and the emotional development—others.

biological mother, who is not constituted to connect the children. This is probably an occurrence of disorganized relationship attachment [36]. Mentally or physically weaker siblings form a coalition in the foster home against the stronger sibling and

Codes	Camp love; good director—but she split me and brother up as a punishment, she sent him to a different city; I do not like my sister because I have not been with her since when I was small; she can punish us, because she likes to; I have a best friend in blue shirt (does not know his name); he likes miss Silvia, the other one likes miss X; sisters are getting on his nerves; professional parent was beating him until he peed himself; then he was beating X and he died; he does not like Maja because of her crossed eyes; he was saying that X was bad (professional foster parent), but no one was listening to; they had to leave his foster family because one of the brother was always hitting people; he hates him now... they packed us up and we had to go... their money disappear; then it was found but they did not take us back...she brought us out things but never came back after that (professional foster mother)... we hid ourselves in the car boot so they cannot take us; if it was not for Mateo they would take us back...; the foster mother hit us sometimes; day and night carers alternate in the children's care home; we always know who has the night shift; the miss that was here when I came has now left... she was here the longest; at school, at summer camp and also outside there are always just kids from foster care.
Categories	Children's home management is perceived by the children as someone who fatalistically decides their fate (to what school they go, how the siblings are split) Children who are in a children's care home since their birth do not have strong bonds to either friends or staff; professional foster parents are perceived as those who require order and discipline and children have learned a lot of activities with them, which they mention with joy; children sensitively register the night staff; They do not understand the context of why they left their families; all kids in the child's surrounding environment are from foster care
Concepts	In some ways, the worker who has been with the children the longest is very important An important role is played by "night workers"—the children perceive them as those who are not employed in the care home as you do not sleep at your place of work. They attribute them a "partial parenthood" Children liked it at professional foster families', but they had a regime, discipline and duties. Although these were limiting them in some ways, they would still prefer to stay there. The children then come to the social environment as an isolated community of children from foster care

Table 5.
Children, their relationships.

fight him actively. The policy of the state, however, states that siblings have to be together. Even in a case of a family with numerous children who do not have any emotional relations among themselves. As it happens, one of the siblings might not be with his behavior accepted by professional or foster family and therefore, has to leave the family. But with him go all the other siblings. The hatred of others towards him only grows on strength. As early as 2010, Bowlby pointed out that there is a higher probability of an unstable emotional connection in children with experience of pathological circumstances in the family and then with the residential environment. This results in different forms of social learning, weaker adoption of family patterns and social skills [37–40]. The antagonism in sibling relationships is supported by the biological parents, grandparents, other relatives, who when visiting, take only one or two children for a walk, because they could not manage more. The frequency of visits is so small, that parents forget which child they took for a walk last time, and end up always taking the child with the least problematic behavior, which only encourages the reciprocal jealousy. When talking to children, an interesting phenomenon has popped up—children "stamp" themselves as well as their siblings. Almost fatalistically they accept that "he takes the bad behavior after mum." Even despite the fact that they have no common family history, that they cannot possible remember what their mother was like. The children accept this sad inheritance in spite of not being able to consider its truthfulness and despite the negative connotation they support it.

Children were not living a harmonious life in their families and since their birth were usually put through many emotional stress situations. The strongest one was for most of them the act of being taken away from the family. Some children went through it many times in their short lives. Children do not know the official reason for being taken away from the family, for which they were put into that particular foster home, or professional family. So they think by themselves, or they take over the arguments from older sibling, roommate or an angry employee. They carry the stigma of the "one who made problems their whole life."

Children, who did not grow up in a family but have been "institutionalized" since birth, create only very vague relationships. They do not even know the name of their best friend (that one in the red shirt), they do not know what they get from which employee, they live through the changes in roommates completely smoothly—as in a hospital, one leaves, and another comes. Exactly the aspect of "at the moment" situation is the most important in their living; children do not plan their life ahead.

The relationship with their biological or foster parents is built mostly on how the child leaves the family. Children have the tendency to apologize the parents from the failure to raise children. They are constantly being let down by false promises of their parents about being taken home, buying them a new phone, taking them shopping or to a restaurant and so on. It functions on the same mechanism as an addiction. The cycle of hope alternates with feelings of hopelessness.

When creating a model of hypothetical ideal home and in forming images of their own future, the children have completely refused their parents and erased them completely from their imaginary. If the child had not an easy time living with his family, he creates only quick and shallow human relationships which the child leaves with the same easiness. The child often changes persons on which he fixates and disengages with the smallest and the pettiest impulse [41–43].

Their parents do not believe in their own parental competencies and it would be the best for them to just visit their children right in the building of the foster home or they would take the children to a restaurant or playground that is the nearest to the foster home. The children like to flaunt others with the fact that somebody came to visit them, on the other side they miss the feeling of having their parents just for themselves. Parents, very childishly, promise attractive things. Both parents and their children in foster home know will never come true. Despite that, the disappointment and hope are two most frequented emotions the child feels towards his parents. The child knows that the parent is lying, but still he defends the parent from himself but mostly from others, and always believes to be consequently disappointed.

The great advantage for the child and the staff is if the children stay in contact with their biological family. These impulses from the side of relatives bring up false hope (maybe he will take me) which results in the disappointment of the child. On the other hand, it increases the confidence of the child and his "value" in the eyes of other children in the foster home that have no contact whatsoever with their relatives. The children can very categorically define their "non-love" towards parents, but would not say the reason for the world. The children who left their family for very dramatic reasons have built a basis for creating and keeping the relationships with other people. These children usually have a person at the foster home or in the close surroundings that they like, seek when they have problems or when they are sad: janitor, auntie in a home, Patrik. Even according to the author Roháček [44], traumas of children in foster care can also be induced by the alternation of educators, the existence of working time, etiquetation, and a lower emotional engagement.

The life in professional families is perceived by the foster children as good in principal, but they "had to" work a lot there. Only after further conversation we have realized that children in professional families usually did only what the children living in functional biological families do. Only in confrontation with the regime approach of the foster home the children felt, like they have to work a lot. They appreciated, that they learnt some concrete skills in professional families and these they take as their own virtues. Leaving the professional family have not been consulted at all with them, therefore they make their own wrong cognitive schemes.

The relationship of children towards things has several specifications as well. The children at foster home have shared stuff. That is common in biological families as well. But besides shared stuff has each member of the family their own personal stuff. Presents from sponsors are given to the children from foster home–ergo, to all of them. The only "other" thing the child can buy for himself either from his very humble pocket money or gets it from relatives. The pocket money is usually spent on sweets. If the parent or the grandparent manages to give something to the child for birthday or Christmas, the thing functions as an attraction, mainly for other children at the foster home. It should support character, privilege and uniqueness of the gifted. But with time children stop envying, because the thing becomes banal. The gift loses its value, so after a very short period of time it is damaged or thrown among other toys at the foster home. Because the children do now experience the ownership of things, they cannot build their "ownership" to people. It is even better to say that relationship building is very flat, shallow short-termed. The value of owned things is insignificant for the child with which is also connected the non/living of the sense of responsibility for something. Useful things, such as pyjamas, undergarment, pens and pencil cases and other, are not chosen by smaller children, but are bought by the staff of the foster home together. Therefore, even the things for children look like "foster" and loose on individuality. Because the children only seldom participate actively on running the household of the foster home, they have no real idea that the rent and energies have to be paid. All of the children would like to live in a house when they grow up, because one must pay for a flat! The older children wait for being 15 years old so that they can find a part-time job and buy whatever they want from the money they will earn.

5.4 Capability 7

Practical thinking is option to create goodness, actively plan one's life, option to realize one's own plans **Table 6**.

5.5 Capability 8

Other living creatures are to have the option to relive the relationship with animals, plants **Table 7**.

In view of the results of the analysis, we have decided to include this capability, albeit in a slightly altered form. Very specific is the relationship of children to things that are not living.

5.6 Capability 9

Game is option to play, entertain and relax **Table 8**.

5.7 Capability 10

Control over one's own environment is to have the right to engage, associate and protect one's own work, as well as to own a property **Table 9**.

For the children is somehow very important the fact how long a member of staff works at the foster home. Senior staff is preferred more, although that does

Codes	Have a normal family; not seven children; have a peaceful life; family home—no need to pay the rent; silence; few children; I teach them to do something; have dogs; certainly not to my mother; to live with my mother and sister, but not with my brothers; he does not know what will be after he leaves the children's home; wants to stay in the city, close to the children's home; wants to keep dogs and owls; does not want any children; wants to be a painter; she wants to be a baker—her sister too (not really); he would like to be a chef on a ship and make a lot of money (in fact, he does not even cook and he does not like it); wants to be a cop; she does not know what she's going to do—she's talking to a psychologist; wants to go to the capital—there's a lot of chances for life; he does not want a family; he will return to his children's home to see his friends (he does not understand passing of time); to see his small brothers; she wants to have three kids but with only one man
Categories	The image of the ideal home certainly does not include the birth parents or a lot of children; the profession of a chef is popular among the children, because this school is attended by many foster care children and you can make good money on a ship; if they say that they cook in the children's care home, it is only because they can be alone with "the miss" in the kitchen and they have her all for themselves in that moment; living in a family home, because they consider this being without costs; they will be returning to the children's care home (time factor)
Concepts	Children fatalistically accept their life and professional career—someone more powerful (children's care home management) has already planned it for them and they are able to accept it without questioning it The concepts of one's own family relate to none or maybe 1–2 children with a stable partner living in a quiet and peaceful family home

Table 6.
Ideas and plans for the future.

Codes	He got a bike from his auntie, it is only his and no one else can take it—he does not know where it is now; she got a doll from her mum (loves her), she took its head off and then legs; there are still other dolls in the children's home; I share a wardrobe with my sister; she does not have anything that is just hers; everything is ours; she does not want anything that's only hers—what for?; mum has promised to buy them a mobile phone; she will be calling a baby to Austria with it; the godfather is nice, he bought a pistol for him, but he threw it away; if a roof is broken in a family house, a repairman comes and he does it for free because he is a repairman; they would like some money for soda; she got a microphone for Christmas, but she does not know where it is anymore; her mother has bought her pyjamas, she only has one pair, but there are a lot of others in the drawer and so she will take a different one; if the bike gets broken a new one will be bought
Categories	Children get things from the people they care about; for a while, these gifts make them feel special, but then they do not matter at all; money is of great value to them, because they bring short-term pleasures; they are not aware of the running costs of a home
Concepts	Children do not bond with things just as they do not bond with people. They are unable to define their own "self" against other children, not even through material things

Table 7.
Relationship to material things.

not mean he is liked more. Maybe, there is a certain form of assurance in it. An important person for the children is the night worker, even though same six workers switch regularly. In a way it can mean for the children that when the staff comes during the day, they are employees at a job (everyone works during the day), but the night shift means they are "coming home."

The children do cleaning chores without objections, but in food preparation they participate only little and sporadically. They perceive it more as an opportunity to have a worker besides only for themselves during cooking. From aunties and nursemaids the children receive some instructions to fulfill their duties, but at the same time they know that these would not check properly upon them, therefore the children do not take them seriously. However, this results also in social habits not being

Codes	They will be with their sister during the holidays (she is in a boarding school)—only the two of us here in care; they will go to a summer camp; the children's care home will be locked and all of us go to a summer camp—everyone from care; they do not want to go home to their parents; from one summer camp to another one; up to three different camps during one summer holiday; mostly there are just kids from foster care; I look forward to the pool and water at summer camp; he goes with the brothers that he does not like; she and her sister play as doctors and the other one wants to play as well, she is ruining the game for them; Christmas is a holiday when school is off and there are fairy tales in television; after school they are running around on the children's home's yard; if the bike is not broken, they ride it; they play football; the nice night shift miss lets them go on computer; they watch football on it and play games
Categories	Children spend the summer at camps; over the year they run around children's care home and the yard there; they do not attend any after school activities; everywhere there are just "foster" kids around; they do not want to go to their parents'; Christmas has the importance of free time and fairy tales watching
Concepts	During the school year children spend their free time running around the children's care home and its yard without a proper focus or a goal. The staff take holidays during the summer, the children's care home is being renovated and in the meantime the children are sent to summer camps. They again spend the time in the closed communities of children from foster care

Table 8.
Entertainment, play, and free time in the children's care home.

Codes	In the children's care home no one is restricting me; if it's our turn we clean up; we do not cook; we do not do the shopping; I can do laundry; there is a miss here who has been with me since I was little; we have freedom—I can go, but I have to tell; I am not being hungry; I can ask for stuff and they give me; I get some allowance but I spend it straightaway; we usually study in the canteen at a table; the menu us at the office with the social worker; dirty clothes go to the bathroom; torn clothes go to the miss; he spends his allowance on soda and sweets and then it's gone!; it is always so loud in the children's home, a lot of shouting, a lot of children; things for hygiene are bought by the misses; at the social worker's office there are locked photos, birth certificates—they allow me there if I want; I always know which night staff is on shift; one cannot eat what one wants—they always make a menu for a whole week; the regime here is terrible; I would not change anything here; I would like to have freedom
Categories	The children will obey the scheduled shifts for cleaning and serving planned meals according to the weekly menu; they would like to get more money to buy more sweets—however they do not complain about the system for allowances; they do not like to noise made by other children in the home, sometimes even the regime, but they cannot really imagine a different way of life
Concepts	The children fatally accept the regime of the social institution and they do not actively fight it. In an increase of their financial income they see a promise of freedom—mainly in how much they can buy from it. They are unable to make use of a freedom in experience, as once the regime relaxes a little, they instantly get bored

Table 9.
Life in a children's care home.

confirmed in their behavior. Dixon and Stein [45], Stein [46, 47] also suggest that the probability of homelessness in children from foster care is rising by the absence of practical skills in obtaining housing, by the presence of debts, or by inadequate relationships with the roommates. Lukšík et al. [48], also Lukšík and Lukšíková [49] emphasizes the importance of stability and continuity of the system as a basic tool in preventing homelessness of young people from foster care. An interesting fact is that the children to not perceive negatively having always to accommodate to new. They are only disturbed by a great amount of screaming children and "it gets on their nerves." The life in the foster home seems like too organized, therefore restricting. They cannot use an occasional freedom (freer regime during holidays) to their own advantage and usually they become bored. The foster home is perceived as one big small world. The same people live in it. The same people are at home, at school, those same attend summer camp, and those same children play outside on the playground. They "rely" only on themselves.

In the hypothetical model of an ideal picture of their own home the children cannot or will not imagine their own parents. A normal home, according to their imagination, looks like this: in a family house (for which one does not have to pay) lives a family with one, two children max. In no case they would let their biological parents "inside" this ideal world not even when they idealize their parents on the outside.

All want to leave the foster home once and live somewhere else. The answer for the question where would they return from the world is the foster home. But they wish to find only friends there, ignoring the time shift. After our objection, that those same friends will grow up and leave, they say they would then return back to their siblings.

Identity has been the last category that is more or less connected with all the basic capabilities. The most problematic seems to be the absence of an individual approach towards children, living in the foster home. We have noticed a weak ability of self-reflection up to non-criticism towards real abilities, which can probably be the result of defenses. The children are non-critical towards their real abilities even when they did not try out the stated activity. With the reaction from the surroundings outside of the foster home they go into defense, because in reality they are usually the aim of attack or laugh for their social background. They are not lead to, and no one guides them, to learn how to endure confrontation, to accept it as a challenge for their further growth and not as another proof of their failure. All this leads to a strange type of behavior, to which children from the "normal" population do not know how to react properly, thus the "fosters" get back to isolation. Fico and his research team has found [34], that in the area of social identity, a child can be labeled a "foster child" or "state child," which then can act as a barrier while searching for housing, or prospective employment. Their personal stuff are locked in a locker of a social worker, because they would lose them. Their personal identity takes on the identity of the room where they live in.

Most of the children is not able to anchor in firmer relationships. Younger children presented their regressive desires. The living through unprocessed sadness is cured by anger and aggression.

The children do not build their own career, they only passively accept their fate and when they reach the adulthood, they lose the restricted assurances and cannot lead their own life. In a better case, one enters the foster home midway (prolongation of the problem) or ends up on the streets.

6. Conclusions

The aim of this chapter was to describe the research findings about the life of children living in the foster home of the so-called family type, considering the phenomenon of capability. We have stemmed from the theoretical concept of Martha Nussbaum and her 10 capabilities, out of which we have followed only five. The challenge for us was to search for the capability at the foster home of family type and we wanted to see how can this state institution ensure such a life for the children they would want and could live?

We dare to make some references at the end. However, we are not entirely sure that we form these references again only from the point of view of adults who know the best what is good for the children.

Child must experience at least for a while functioning in a family. Otherwise, the child knows nothing about sharing tasks, roles, and does not experience the feeling of responsibility—for himself, for things, animals or people. Only then the child is able to form lasting relationships. If the child must leave the family, someone must talk with him about it, analyze his part in this act and help him understand it. Teach the children to decide systematically and take responsibility for decisions. The absence of responsibility is a phenomenon they acquire from their biological family.

The child cannot live in two residencies at the same time. This way overrides the adaptive skills of any one the siblings, who for various reasons do not feel their family affiliation, cannot be force to relive it, so that feelings of guilt and anger towards sibling will not stem from it. Family identity should get a chance, but not a forced one, because one can repair only what truly exists.

The share of the children on household chores should be higher, in a case the staff is occupied, the volunteers should be brought in. First and foremost, with the imitation of others they would learn about "household," about spending free time. Their abilities to live their own life are developed this way and the children would not fall into hopelessness of not being able to live without organizing their life by the foster home or other social "greenhouse."

The child should get, considering his options and skills, an individual care, so that the personal identity of an individual is developed instead of the identity of the "foster." We should build child's personality more and support a positive confidence and self-evaluation and teach the child self-reflection, so that he does not become a laughing stock outsider of the society.

Help parents and profit parents, and other relatives, to handle visits of children, written contacts with children and short visits in a way that does not scare them and they would not end the contact with children from the fear of offices returning their children back into their care and them not handling it that well again.

It would be interesting to research the perception of time dimension, as well as the ability of self-reflection in children living in a residential care.

Our chapter has been called mirage. The image, that a very tired person sees somewhere in the distance and one just needs to take one step and all will be fine. Such a mirage is a family for the children living in the foster homes of family type. An image, that vanishes into thin air.

Acknowledgements

The author disclosed receipt of the following financial support for the research, authorship, and/or publication of this chapter. This chapter was created with the support of the Grant of Slovak Research and Development Agency APVV N. 16-0205 titled Identification of mechanisms for early diagnosis CAN syndrome.

Conflict of interest

The author of this chapter declared no potential conflicts of interest with respect to the research, authorship, and/or publication of this chapter.

Author details

Eva Mydlíková
Trnava University, Trnava, Slovakia

*Address all correspondence to: eva.mydlikova@truni.sk

References

[1] Opis projektu deinštitucionalizácie náhradnej rodinnej starostlivosti [Internet]. 2007. Available from: https://www.upsvr.gov.sk/buxus/docs/download/OPIS_NP_DEI_SR.rtf [Accessed: 10 December 2018]

[2] Počet detí mimo vlastnej rodiny [Internet]. 2016. Available from: https://www.upsvr.gov.sk/buxus/docs/SSVaR/OVOZ/statisticke_ukazovtele/Pocet_deti_mimo_vlastnej_rodiny.pdf [Accessed: 28 November 2018]

[3] Zákon o sociálnoprávnej ochrane detí a sociálnej kuratele [Internet]. 2018. Available from: https://www.slov-lex.sk/pravne-predpisy/SK/ZZ/2005/305/20180401 [Accessed: 14 December 2018]

[4] Ben-Arieh A. Beyond welfare: Measuring and monitoring the state of children—New trends and domains. Social Indicators Research. 2000;**52**(3):235-257

[5] Biggeri M, Santi M. The missing dimensions of children's well-being and well-becoming in education systems: Capabilities and philosophy for children. Journal of Human Development and Capabilities. 2012;**13**(3):373-395. DOI: 10.1080/19452829.2012.694858

[6] Beck U. Riziková společnost. Praha: Slon; 2004. p. 431

[7] Navrátil P, Navrátilová J. Postmodernita jako prostor pro existenciálně citlivou sociální práci. Časopis sociální práce/Sociálna práca. 2008;**8**(4):124-135

[8] Ventegodt S, Merrick J, Andersen NJ. Quality of life theory I. The IQOL theory: An integrative theory of the global quality of life concept. The Scientific World Journal. 2003;**3**:1030-1040. DOI: 10.1100/tsw.2003.82

[9] Ventegodt S, Merrick J, Andersen NJ. Quality of life theory III. Maslow revisited. The Scientific World Journal. 2003;**3**:1050-1057. DOI: 10.1100/tsw.2003.84

[10] Sirgy MJ. A quality-of-life theory derived from Maslow's developmental perspective. American Journal of Economics and Sociology. 2006;**45**(3):329-342. DOI: 10.1111/j.1536-7150.1986.tb02394.x

[11] Ben-Arieh A. Measuring and monitoring the well-being of young children around the world. Paper commissioned for the EFA Global Monitoring Report 2007, strong foundations: Early childhood care and education [Internet]. 2007. Available from: https://unesdoc.unesco.org/ark:/48223/pf0000147444 [Accessed: 10 December 2018]

[12] Ben-Arieh A. From child welfare to children well-being: The child indicators perspective. In: Kamerman SB, Phipps S, Ben-Arieh A, editors. From Child Welfare to Child Well-Being. An International Perspective on Knowledge in the Service of Policy Making. London: Springer; 2010. pp. 9-22. DOI: 10.1007/978-90-481-3377-2

[13] Ben-Arieh A, Kaufma NH, Andrews AB, George RM, Lee B, Aber LJ. Measuring and Monitoring children's Well-Being. Berlin: Springer Science & Business Media; 2013. p. 153. DOI: 10.1007/978-94-017-2229-2

[14] O'Hara M, Lyon A. Well-being and well-becoming: Reauthorizing the subject in incoherent times. In: Hämäläinen TH, Michaelson J, editors. Well-Being and beyond: Broadening the Public and Policy Discourse. Camberley Surrey: Edward Elgar Publishing; 2014. pp. 98-122

[15] Navrátilová J. Využití capability přístupu při posouzení dětského well-beingu. Czech and Slovak Social Work/Sociální Práce/Sociálna Práca. 2018;**5**:65-77

[16] Sen A. Capability and well-being. In: Nussbaum M, Sen A, editors. The Quality of Life. Oxford Scholarship Online; 1993. p. 30. DOI: 10.1093/0198287976.001.0001

[17] Sen A. Capabilities, lists, and public reason: Continuing the conversation. Feminist Economics. 2004;**10**(3):77-80. DOI: 10.1080/1354570042000315163

[18] Sen A. Human rights and capabilities. Journal of Human Development. 2005;**6**(2):151-166. DOI: 10.1080/14649880500120491

[19] Nussbaum MC, Sen A, editors. The Quality of Life. Oxford: Oxford University Press; 1993. DOI: 10.1093/0198287976.001.0001

[20] Nussbaum MC. Capabilities and human rights. Fordham Law Review. 1997;**66**(2):273

[21] Nussbaum MC. Women and Human Development. The Capabilities Approach. Cambridge: Cambridge University Press; 2000. p. 312

[22] Nussbaum MC. Frontiers of Justice: Disability, Nationality, Species Membership. Cambridge, Massachusetts, London: The Belknap Press: An Imprint of Harvard University Press; 2007. p. 512

[23] Roybens I. The capability approach: A theoretical survey. Journal of Human Development. 2005;**6**(1):93-117. DOI: 10.1080/146498805200034266

[24] Berelson B. Content Analysis in Communication Research. New York: Free Press; 1952. p. 220

[25] Schreier M. Qualitative Content Analysis in Practice. London: SAGE; 2012. p. 280

[26] Mayring P. Qualitative content analysis. Forum Qualitative Sozialforschung/Forum: Qualitative Social Research. 2000;**1**(2):20. DOI: 10.17169/fqs-1.2.1089

[27] Hendl J. Kvalitativní výzkum. 2. vyd. ed. Praha: Portál; 2008. 408 s

[28] Strauss A, Corbinová J. Základy kvalitativního výzkumu. 1. vyd. ed. Boskovice: Nakladatelství Albert; 1999. 228 s

[29] Prokša M, Held Ľ. Metodológia pedagogického výskumu a jeho aplikácia v didaktikách prírodných vied. 1. vyd. ed. Bratislava: Univerzita Komenského v Bratislave; 2008. 229 s

[30] Švaříček R, Šeďová K. a kol. Kvalitativní výzkum v pedagogických vědách. 1. vyd. ed. Praha: Portál; 2007. 377 s

[31] Pavelek L. Zakotvená teória (GROUNDED THEORY) a možnosti jej použitia v oblasti sociálnej práce. [Internet]. 2012. Available from: http://lukaspavelek.blogspot.sk/2011/04/pdf.html [Accessed: 18 November 2012]

[32] Sprod T. "Nobody really knows": The structure and analysis of social constructivist whole class discussions. International Journal of Science Education. 1997;**19**(8):911-924. DOI: 10.1080/0950069970190805

[33] Gavora P. Obsahová analýza v pedagogickom výskume: Pohľad na jej súčasné podoby. Pedagogická orientace. 2015;**25**(3):345-371. DOI: 10.5817/PedOr2015-3-345

[34] Fico M. Práca s deťmi v detských Domovoch a Ich pracovné Uplatnenie po Odchode So zameraním na Aktivity, ktoré Sa s deťmi realizujú v Detskom Domove [Internet]. 2017. Available from: https://www.ceit.sk/IVPR/images/IVPR/vyskum/2017/Fico/dd_iprod_zamestnanost.pdf [Accessed: 28 November 2018]

[35] Juhásová A. Životné perspektívy mladých dospelých po ukončení pobytu

v detskom domove. Grant Journal. 2016;**5**(1):32-36

[36] Main M, Solomon J. Procedures for identifying infants as disorganized/disoriented during the Ainsworth strange situation. In: Greenberg MT, Cicchetti D, Cummings EM, editors. The John D. And Catherine T. MacArthur Foundation Series on Mental Health and Development. Attachment in the Preschool Years: Theory, Research, and Intervention. Chicago. IL, US: University of Chicago Press; 1990. pp. 121-160

[37] Vazba BJ. Teorie kvality vztahů mezi matkou a dítětem. Praha: Portál; 2010. 360 s

[38] Bowlby J. Odloučení. Kritické období raného vztahu mezi matkou a dítětem. Praha: Portál; 2012. 400 s

[39] Hughes DA. Facilitating Developmental Attachment: The Road to Emotional Recovery and Behavioral Change in Foster and Adopted Children. New York: Jason Aronson, Inc.; 1997. p. 276

[40] Landy S. Pathway to Competence. Baltimore: Paul H. Brookes Publishing; 2002. 672 p

[41] Bretherton I. The origins of attachment Theory. John Bowlby and Mary Ainsworth. In: Golberg S, Muir R, Kerr J, editors. Attachment Theory. Social, Developmental and Clinical Perspectives. New York: Routledge; 2000. pp. 45-84

[42] Cassidy J. The nature of the Child's ties. In: Cassidy J, Shaver PR, editors. Handbook of Attachment. Theory, Research, and Clinical Applications. 2nd ed. New York: The Guilford Press; 2008. pp. 3-22

[43] Van IJzendoorn MH. Adult attachment representations, parental responsiveness, and infant attachment: A meta-analysis on the predictive validity of the adult attachment interview. Psychological Bulletin. 1995;**117**(3):387-403

[44] Roháček M. Profesionálny rodič alebo guľatá kocka, Sprievodca profesionálnou náhradnou výchovou v rodine, Návrat. [Internet]. 2000. Available from: http://www.navrat.sk/data/files/publikacie/Profesionalny_rodic_alebo_gulata_kocka.pdf [Accessed: 18 November 2012]

[45] Dixon J, Stein M. Leaving Care, Troughcare and Aftercare in Scotland. London: Jessica kingsley; 2005. p. 192

[46] Stein M. Research review: Zoung people leaving care, child and family social work. Child & Family Social Work. 2006;**11**(3):273-279. DOI: 10.1111/j.1365-2206.2006.00439.x

[47] Stein M. Young People Leaving Care. Supporting Pathways to Adulthood. London: Jessica Kingsley Publishers; 2012. 200 p

[48] Lukšík I. Rezidenciálna reziliencia—kontextuálna povaha psychologických konštruktov. In: Komunitná psychológia na Slovensku, 2 Decembra 2014. Bratislava, UK: Fakulta sociálnych a ekonomických vied; 2014. pp. 53-62

[49] Lukšík I, Lukšíkova Ľ. Starať sa o seba v ústavnej starostlivosti. In: Hudečková V, Byndzák P, Škoviera A, editors. Regulácia a sebaregulácia v prevýchove. Zborník z medzinárodnej konferencie Križovatky VI, 16-17 Októbra. 2014. Bratislava: Diagnostické centrum Záhorská Bystrica/FICE; 2015. pp. 55-61

Section 3

Specific Topics

Chapter 7

Family Therapy: When the Adolescents' Discourse is the Principal Resource

Silvia Renata Lordello

Abstract

Family therapy with adolescent children may greatly benefit from the narrativist approach. In this chapter clinical cases will be presented in which stories told by adolescents and their families gain a prominent place in therapy, allowing stories saturated with problems to undergo an effective process of re-signification, reorganization of experience, and re-authorization. The cases presented will illustrate how externalization exercises and re-authorships can be rich tools for psychotherapy. Another aspect addressed will be the therapist's posture, in which the therapist is always open to dialog and willing to learn from the client, who is the greatest expert on their demands.

Keywords: adolescence, family therapy, narrative perspective, externalization, re-authorship

1. Introduction

Family therapy has undergone many changes in recent decades. Inspired by the early movements of Gregory Bateson and his work with families of schizophrenics, many new ideas and theories have been incorporated. Such innovations have been transformative and contribute to the growth of a form of psychotherapy that, since its origin, has been guided by complexity and nonlinearity. Thus, this chapter aims to address two of these innovations in family therapy: the adolescents' contribution to the understanding of family scenario in this life cycle and the use of dialogic and discursive resources in the family therapeutic process.

To illustrate the dialogical perspective in clinical practice and active participation of adolescents in family psychotherapy, clinical cases from Brazil's public schools' service will be used. The adolescents' families looked for new vacancies on the service-school attendance, due to being a service directed to the low-income public, with symbolic fees. The family, when seeking the service, is aware that the psychological sessions are conducted by trainee therapists under the supervision of a doctoral professor, specialist in systemic family psychotherapy, who develops therapeutic work based on postmodern conceptions. For ethical reasons, the names presented in the text are fictitious, avoiding any identification.

2. Plural teens and a new understanding for clinical intervention

The contemporary family experiences the challenge of absorbing the demands of society and the relationships that constitute them, needing to reinvent itself. Considering the contexts in which this process is inserted, it is continuous and complex, as the transformations in the sociohistorical scenario are fast and modify the relational patterns [1]. When the family passes through the moment of the adolescence of the children, this dynamism and reorganization of papers become even more evident.

According to Brazilian authors who specialized in studying family in the life cycle, adolescent phase is the period in which family experiences the transition from childhood to adolescence [2]. This children to adolescence transition usually promotes a recrudescence from its own dilemmas and a reprint of the internalized youth itself. It is a phase of family self-regulation, in which parents and children redefine their roles, and there is a new rhythm in the family, which should also allow the process of differentiation as a way of building the identity of adolescents. It is a period marked by new researches, existential meanings, and empowerment of new roles which are both within the family and also in the particularity of each spouse, which can occur even when the couple does not have children.

As for the relationship between parents and children, there are several peculiarities. The first one is, because of the identity's sense construction, the processes of differentiation require the characteristic of opposition to the adults, which until then had been a model for adolescents. This necessary opposition is confused with rebellion and receives much reproach from parents, who misinterpret it as an attack at their authority.

The parents' view of adolescence originates in culture, which diffuses it as a difficult period, with universal and deterministic characteristics, which aim to provide a single view to understand all adolescents, devaluing the potential of the phase. This distortion is reproduced by the media and naturalized by society, contributing to a social reading that minimizes and delegitimizes adolescents' experiences [2].

Developmental psychology has collaborated to broaden these visions, showing that sociocultural differences make the adolescence a multifaceted concept. In addition to the remarkable physical transformations, it is a period of global development, which includes the construction of the identity and the meaning of the subject's life and the experimentation of new roles that emerge in a context of gaining autonomy and changes in sociocultural ties [3].

According to a Brazilian researcher [4], the experiences in this stage of life can be comprehended as essays, which are provisional ones or definitive ones. Intervention and social support are the differentials that guarantee the possibility of approaching and moving away from situations and roles during adolescent trials, without them being permanent or deterministic in the other stages of the person's life cycle. Considering this vision of plural adolescents and the importance of families understanding the richness of this period in all its complexity to stimulate autonomy and recognition of adolescent potentialities, the chapter adopts the narrative referential as an important therapeutic resource, which we describe.

3. Postmodern conceptions and co-construction of the family psychotherapeutic process

The review of the original concepts of family therapy, which emphasized cybernetics, circularity, and communicational aspects, has provided the rescue of the individual dimension and of narratives as a construction of the personal and contextual meaning of experience [5–7]. From this perspective, social constructionism was chosen as an epistemological current capable of favoring access and understanding of the narratives, qualifying the experience of psychotherapy of adolescents with a family approach. Social constructionism provides a favorable view of complex phenomena, as it presupposes the centrality of language and relationships in the construction of knowledge, the emphasis on local and historically situated character, and the understanding of knowledge as a form of social action [8].

When referring to social constructionism, some derivations are mentioned, such as the collaborative approach, described in detail by Anderson and Golishian: the narrative therapy, originally present in the studies of White and Epston; and the reflective processes mentioned in the works of Andersen. The adoption of the collaborative approach is positively evaluated by the family members in different studies, which highlight the change from an individual understanding of the problem to a relational view and the collaborative construction of the solution, previously delegated to the therapist. Gergen and Gergen emphasize the link between action and meanings, advocating that constructionist work favors the process of becoming aware of what is being narrated and involves decisions about life choices [9–12].

The framework that underlies the clinical practice to be presented will bring some specificities of the narrative approach of White, a postmodern school whose contribution is visible when considering psychotherapy as a resource for the re-signification of each person's relationships and understandings about himself, a the other, and on the world. In clinical practice, the search for expansion of perspectives by updating the narratives brought to each session is noticed [13].

4. Uses of dialogic and discursive resources in family therapy

The postmodern chains of family therapy propose a position in which the construction of reality takes place through the language and social processes of which we are actors. This attitude of being in a conversation, in dialog with oneself and with others, represents openness to new possibilities since meanings and understandings are interpreted, reinterpreted, clarified, and revised.

The dialog dimension and the collaborative practice in therapy are widely defended by Anderson [14]. On this author thought, it is in the dialog dimension as dynamic, relational and generative processes that the possibility of transformation resides. She understands the relationship between therapists and clients such as conversational partners, which is a genuine exchange, improves understandings, and amplifies meanings, in a compromise opposite to the search for consensual and unique truth. The conversational partners' interest is not to search what was not discovered but to look at what is familiar following new readings, new meanings, and innovative joints with the contexts that are inserted. This collaborative activity, which rejects the prejudgments and is sincerely interested in others, is appreciated in the family therapy with adolescents, and achieving this dialogical and affective availability among the members is quite challenging.

In family therapy with adolescents, it is understood that as communication issues are always demanded in clinical care, this approach is promising to work on. With some fragments of cases attended in our community service, we will be able to elucidate.

Maria, a 15-year-old teenager, was accompanied by her mother, Ana, and her only 13-year-old sister, Nataly, and they entered the clinical setting a lot mobilized in their first consultation. The therapist welcomed them, and in an open and interested manner, she was receptive to the way they wanted to express the contents which brought them there. Her mother revealed she felt very sorry for raising teenage girls without a father and without any help and soon said she felt exhausted with the demands of her daughters because in adolescence they changed and only irritated her with their disobedience. Maria described some symptoms that made her look for the service: deep sadness and shame to express herself, to the point of getting prejudice in several fields. The mother said that she felt responsible for this, since she was depressed, sad, and shared this suffering with her daughters. Maria disagreed that this contributed to her image. The mother stated that she "spoke for her daughter" (sic) and that this was a problem and Maria and Nataly agreed. In addition, Maria added another content: her need for greater autonomy, with few negotiations in the family environment. Nataly revealed that she feels guilty when her mother says she became a monster after she left her childhood. They were often moved to speak about their sufferings, but it was felt that space gave them relief and they were receptive to psychotherapy.

When analyzing this first clinical session, the presence of many elements expressed by the language was observed. The family therapist, consistent with its theoretical foundation, was concerned with preparing a receptive atmosphere appropriate to inviting family members to dialog. According to Anderson, the dialog is a relational and collaborative activity and fosters a sense of mutuality, of which respect and interest are genuine. This practice encourages clients to take the place of experts on their stories, which empowers them and gives them a different place to the therapist who refuses asymmetrical positions and power [15].

Openness to the family allowed the mother to express her feelings, as well as her daughters to stand and express themselves freely. The first session is dedicated to the evaluation of demands but already shows the productive field of the intervention. It is interesting how it is noticing the macrosystemic elements present in the mother's speech, expressing stereotypes about adolescence, such as those spread by the culture which already brings the opposition outlook associated with disobedience.

The outstanding systemic view is that the client of psychotherapy will not be the mother or the daughters but rather the relationships. Therefore, in the following sessions, the dialogical practice sought to remove individual faults, assumed by the mother in relation to her depression or by her daughters, with its academic and social difficulties to focus on the conversations of externalization. According to White and Epston [16], the purpose of outsourcing practices is for people to realize that the problems and themselves are not diffused. When outsourcing conversations are proposed, there is an exploration of the problem in perspective, covering it by the context in which it was produced, and this allows the outsourced to shift and change over time.

In the case of this family, it was possible to take from the internal degree the depression of the mother, Maria's sadness, and the guilt of her sister for her opposition toward her mother. Thus, it was sought to defuse the problem as a therapeutic centrality and to find extraordinary moments in which a sense of competence has been used to try to solve them. Here is a warning, when it is spoken that it does not focus on the problem, it is not at all not to approach it. Rather, the key element of outsourcing is to explore in detail the actual effect of externalized problems and their effects on people's lives but also to think of alternatives to mitigate their effects and impacts.

In the following sessions, the adolescents played a key role in undertaking another unique narrative feature: re-authorship conversations. Re-authorship involves the identification and co-creation of alternative lines of identity. The therapist's posture is fundamental because it questions research elements that contradict the dominant, problem-saturated history. The re-authorship conversation is based on the assumption that no story can cover the totality of the experiences; there will always be arguments and scenarios that can be created, which open to the transformative possibility of an alternative story. Maria, for example, asked about the sadness and suicidal ideation that paralyzed her, reported that, during the play days at school, she did not feel she was losing and that she could express herself without fear or shame, because of languages such as dance, theater, and music being allowed.

This extraordinary moment, as it is termed theoretically, was extensively explored and, in Maria's case, opened new questions about this new scenario and its connection to other events that were becoming a new history, with successful experiences in its communication. Nataly was able to present the session with moments in which her disobedience had been seen as leadership in the school and her questions and doubts were recognized as a sign of autonomy and protagonist. The mother was also able to reveal that although she was deeply drowned by depression, she could have the strength to work, and she did not skip her job service due to depression, telling some strategies that she used to fight her anhedonia. Outsourcing conversations and detection of extraordinary moments are significant narrative resources since they allow for re-signification and when counting reorganize the experience into temporality and spatiality that may have gone unnoticed at the moment in which the experience was lived.

White [17] developed a map of re-authorship conversations, dividing the questioning into two categories: action scenarios and identity scenarios. The act of mapping Maria's family narratives was extremely useful since there are countless disqualifying attributes: Maria was feeling incapable, the mother was feeling guilty, and her sister was very unhappy with the guilt she carried and the lack of autonomy. Being able to dialog in the sessions on how these narratives were produced, what events and actions were present in those moments, mapping the implications of this for their identity and the identity of those close to them was extremely important for the process of looking back at themselves and the impacts that they caused on the other person.

The mother, for example, reviewed several scenarios in which she did not grant autonomy to her daughters for fear due to the world's violence (action) but understood that the identities could benefit from small concessions of autonomy, such as not speaking for them and allowing them to pay a small freedom that is not linked to security. Thusly, Maria was able to visualize a story that she called "Daily Surpasses for a Better Conquest and Communication." Her mother built her new story with the title "Live and Let Them Live," focusing on strategies for her personal project and incorporating elements of adolescent communication to understand what she felt may have extrapolated into her overprotective attitudes. Finally, the sister, who was also very distressed by the repressive atmosphere in the house, invested in an alternative story in which she played a leading role in her teenage processes.

Another clinical case for illustration is Daniela's, a 14-year-old adolescent whom sought the service by referral from a psychiatric center, showing a phobic-anxious picture. The parents stated they got scared with the daughter's symptoms: fear, panic crisis, despair, and excessive worry with diseases. In the first session, the adolescent has shown dizziness, nausea, sweatiness, and shivering; in addition, she had problems to sleep, which led to the consumption of psychotropic drugs with medical accompaniment. The adolescent felt paralyzed and wasn't able to get back to her daily activities and went to the first attendance with her father, José; her mother, Helena; and her 17-year-old brother. The family was willing to help but felt impotent through Daniela's suffering.

In a social constructive perspective, the first step was to rethink Daniela's diagnostic in the light of family perceptions. Adopting the conception from Anderson and Golishian [18], in which the client is the specialist, conceding the voice toward the family's members to translate its emotions and its resources allowed to replace the pathology of a member by a process of co-responsibility from all family members. This has favored conversations which allowed to create new bonds and connections [19].

The narrative therapist, through their dialogical posture, invited the whole family to contemplate the problem in an alternative way, not painful, with sincere interest in the perceptions about the construction of this picture and making use of sincere questionings, in an ambient of complete exemption from judgments.

The participation by Daniela and her brother was very significant to the following of the therapeutic process, as its adolescence stories pointed to a family context which intimidated process of differentiation. Over the narratives it was noticed that Daniela was sleeping in her parent's bed who have offered this admeasurement to protect their daughter from her fears. The brother revealed his intense familiarity with cyber means, being highly repudiated from his parents. This parents' duty put in the children was also revised in its transgerational dimension, once it was a common behavior in the past generations.

The narrative therapist was very capable in questioning, as the externalization has set Daniela free from being guilty and responsible for what she felt. According to Morgan [20], the manners which are understood in our lives are influenced by the wide views from the history of the culture in which we live. Daniela's diagnostic was rethought in the light of our culture that often incites the search of pathology in human beings. The externalization conversations weaken the effects of the diagnostic label and of the pathologization, as it separates the person from the problem itself. In this form, externalization decreases the unproductive conflict around the problem and evokes cooperation and collaboration, since the problem gives up from being concentrated in one identity.

5. Conclusions

Family therapy has benefited from innovations that postmodernity has been demanding. By having a tradition which breaks the linearity and predicts the complexity as a lens to the phenomena comprehension, collaborative and dialog postures in therapy have shown to be appropriate to quickly change context that families are being subjected. The adolescents, as family members, show up quite receptive to a therapeutic approach in which they can tell their stories because they are immediately affected by a world whose technological and social changes are quickly felt.

Shotter [21] states that as much as experiences are qualitatively different, they are always available for being nominated in several forms. With the word choices for them to be nominated, comes to the fore relations and connections with other experiences beyond the possibilities to act in the future. The family therapy with adolescents is an excellent opportunity to build safe spaces, so that different experiences and perspectives may have a place without compromise in search of truth or a consensual thought. The adolescents easily accept this invite, and in a spontaneous condition, they tell their truths, with their vocabulary, contextualized in their world and, there so, stimulate adults to do the same.

Narrating stories in the therapeutic context can be an excellent form to enter in contact with the circumstances in which these stories were built. Often, narratives focus on problem and symptoms. The narrative therapist worries in amplifying the strict descriptions, which obscure the meanings; thereby, they do not guide limiting and imprisoning conclusions. In this case, the therapeutic work seeks to request, create conversations, and identify histories which help people build alternative routes to the problems they are impacting.

The process of co-creating these new narratives is not that simple, and that is why re-authorship conversations are not the first step. White names as positioning map the fact that first it is necessary to name the problem, explore its effects, evaluate them, and then justify its evaluations. Challenging beliefs taken as genuine and that provoke the distance from problems are a process of deconstruction; they are beneficial for sitting dominant stories, allowing exploring new perspectives and setting them culturally and historically.

The narrative therapist adopts a relational posture in which it does not impose viewpoints and prefer to be guided through the interest in routes and contents such clients follow to express their narratives. The adolescents, with their typical expressiveness, enrich in abundance the setting, showing a big opening to new possibilities, and bring a colorful creativeness to the alternative stories, applying them immediately in each context. As a conclusion, the desired narrativism in the family-adolescent children therapy should be comprehended as a powerful therapeutic instrumental and full of protagonism.

Author details

Silvia Renata Lordello
University of Brasilia, Brasília, Brazil

*Address all correspondence to: srmlordello@gmail.com

References

[1] Moreira M, Bedran P, Carellos S, Passos A. As famílias e as crianças acolhidas: histórias mal contadas. Psicologia em Revista. 2013;**19**:59-73

[2] Ceverny C, Berthoud C. Ciclo vital na família brasileira. In: Osório L, Valle M, editors. Manual de terapia familiar. Porto Alegre: Artes Médicas; 2009. pp. 25-37

[3] Rodriguez S, Damásio B. O desenvolvimento da identidade e sentido de vida na adolescência. In: Habgzang L, Diniz E, Koller S, editors. Trabalhando com adolescentes. Porto Alegre: Artes Médicas; 2014. pp. 30-41

[4] Carreteiro T. Adolescências e experimentações possíveis. In: Marra M, Costa L, editors. Temas da clínica do adolescente e da família. São Paulo: Ágora; 2010. pp. 15-24

[5] Boscolo L, Bertrando L. Terapia sistêmica individual: manual prático na clínica. Belo Horizonte, Artesã; 2012

[6] Costa L. A perspectiva sistêmica para a clínica de família. Psicologia: Teoria e Pesquisa; 2010. pp. 95-104. DOI: 10.1590/S0102-37722010000500008

[7] Grandesso M. Mapas da prática narrativa. Nova Perspectiva Sistêmica. 2012;**44**:105-107

[8] Barbosa M, Guanaes-Lorenzi C. Sentidos construídos por familiares acerca de seu processo terapêutico em terapia familiar. Psicologia Clínica. 2015;**27**:15-38

[9] Anderson H, Golishian H. O cliente é o especialista: A abordagem terapêutica do não saber. In: Mc Namee S, Gergen J, editors. A terapia como construção social. Porto Alegre: Artes Médicas; 1998. pp. 34-50

[10] White M, Epston D. Narrative Means to Therapeutic Ends. New York: W.W. Norton & Company; 1990

[11] Gergen K, Gergen M. Construcionismo social: um convite ao diálogo. Rio de janeiro: Instituto Noos; 2010

[12] Andersen T. Processos Reflexivos. Rio de Janeiro: Noos; 1999

[13] Marra M. Conversas criativas e abuso sexual: uma proposta para o atendimento psicossocial. São Paulo: Ágora; 2016

[14] Anderson H. Diálogo: pessoas criando significados umas com as outras e encontrando maneiras de seguir adiante. In: Grandesso M, editor. Práticas colaborativas e Dialógicas: distintos contextos e diferentes atuações. Curitiba: CRV; 2017. pp. 93-103

[15] Anderson H. Converstion, Language and Possibilities: A Postmodern Approach to Therapy. New York: Basic Books; 1997

[16] White M, Epston D. Experience, Contradiction, Narrative & Imagination. Adelaide: Dulwich Centre Publications; 1992

[17] White M. Re-authoring. Lives: Interview & Essays. Adelaide: Dulwich Centre Publications; 1995

[18] Anderson H, Golishian H. Sistemas humanos como sistemas linguísticos: implicações ara a teoria clínica e a terapia familiar. In: Grandesso M, editor. Colaboração e Diálogo: aportes teóricos e possibilidades práticas. Curitiba: CRV; 2018. pp. 23-58

[19] Gergen K. Relational Being Beyond Self and Community. New York: Oxford University Press; 2009

[20] Morgan A. O que é terapia narrativa? Porto Alegre: Centro de Estudos e Práticas Narrativas; 2007

[21] Shotter J. Ontological risks and communication anxieties—On what and whom others will 'allow' us to be. International Journal of Collaborative Practice. 2016;**6**(1):1-12

Chapter 8

Group Process as a Resocialization Intervention: The Family - People Helping People Project

David F. Allen, Keva Bethell, Marie Allen-Carroll and Flavia D'Alessandro

Abstract

This chapter presents a cultural adaptation of a group process model as a resocialization project to confront social fragmentation in the Bahamas. The Family: People Helping People Project seeks to improve communication and socialization in New Providence, the capital of the Bahamas. The chapter provides an overview of The Family and addresses key elements along with clinical examples to show the success of the model. We also present the results of a pilot study carried out on The Family which further outlined the benefits of participating in the program. We hope that these insights are helpful in addressing community problems around the world, with the hope of reducing violence and social fragmentation.

Keywords: social fragmentation, resocialization, group process, family, community

1. Introduction

The Bahamas is an archipelagic nation situated between Florida at the southern tip of the United States of America in the north and Cuba in the south. Once a British colony, the Bahamas is now an independent country and an active member of the British Commonwealth. The population is about 400,000 people, with the majority of the persons under 50 years of age. Most of the people are of African descent, and the rest are a mixture of Caucasians from Europe, North America, South America and Canada. The predominant religion is Christianity although there are representatives of other religions such as Hinduism, Islam, Rastafarianism, etc. The major industries are tourism supplemented by international banking and a few farming and fishing enterprises.

Once a pristine, quiet paradise, the Bahamas has undergone a serious social fragmentation process associated with the major country-wide crack cocaine epidemic of the 1980s [1] and its continuing sequelae of drug trafficking, chronic addiction and oversupply of powerful guns. This dissociation is manifested by burgeoning murder and violent crime rates (**Figure 1**) along with high incidences of domestic violence and different forms of child abuse. Crack was the first drug that feminized drug addiction, ejecting mothers from the home, leaving children to fend for themselves. Thus the crack epidemic of the 1980s produced severe family and community disintegration which, combined with the international economic downturn of 2008, led to high youth unemployment and the development of violent gangs

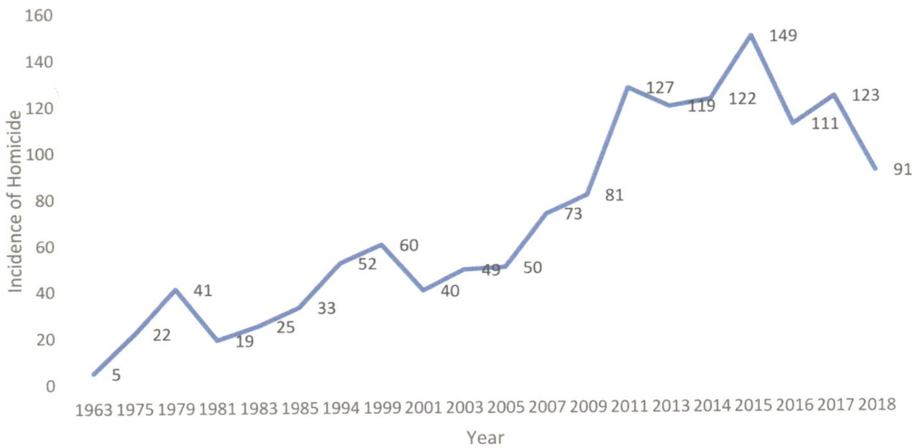

Figure 1.
Incidence of homicide in the Bahamas (1963–2018).

which terrorize the community. According to Shaw and McKay, these areas may be referred to as zones of transition, likely formed by a combination of individual choice and a crime-enhancing environment [2]. This regional culture of violence has adversely affected all levels of Bahamian society and contributes to extensive family and community fragmentation [1].

2. The formation of The Family: People Helping People Project

In 2008, while doing follow-up research on the effects of the 1980s crack cocaine epidemic, my team was confronted with the horrible spectra of community dissocialization. There was no need to describe further the destructive nature of the epidemic. The challenge was to develop some type of community intervention to impact the prevailing social chaos which had destroyed so many pristine and well put together neighborhoods. A review of the literature shows there is much debate on the definition of Social Fragmentation and its counterpart, resocialization [3–5]. In an effort to develop an effective community intervention, Social Fragmentation was defined as a process in which persons, victimized by the negativity of shame, develop a diminished view of themselves and become involved in destructive activities toward themselves and others. Shame, a powerful master emotion, results from the shattering of cherished dreams, hopes and expectations. Covert in nature, shame manifests itself in society as anger, violence, revenge, addiction, intimacy dysfunction, abuse and destructive community relationships [6]. Resocialization, which we refer to as "Discovery," involves the liberation of persons from the negativity of shame by sharing their painful stories in a contemplative atmosphere of mindfulness, acceptance and non-judgmental listening. The release of shame allows persons to experience the positive emotions of love, humility, forgiveness and gratitude, leading to the development of healing community of caring and service.

In light of these concepts, the aim was to develop a resocialization intervention using a community process model. Starting with a small group of seven mothers who had lost their sons to murder, we met weekly to share their painful stories. The expression of the deep, painful feelings of shame and grief in this group of mothers was overwhelming. But during the group process, a powerful healing bond developed among us, enhancing cohesion, empathy and a deep sense of community.

This healing bond was defined as "Family," counteracting the mental health stigmatization of participants being seen as patients or victims. This program developed into The Family: People Helping People Project, known as "The Bahamas Family." Within a year, the group expanded to 30 persons, including relatives of the victims of murder, criminal violence, domestic disputes, multiple types of physical and sexual abuse, and causalities of the international economic collapse. Thus The Family became a powerful group process model, representing a therapeutic replica of the home-based family, allowing members to confront their issues in a safe and non-judgmental environment. Providing support and advocacy for its members, The Family allows persons to discover themselves and grow as individuals. More importantly, The Family offers a sanctuary from normal Bahamian culture, encouraging the expression of emotions that are normally taboo (for example, grief, shame, closeness, love and hope). The primary goal was to improve socialization using the principles of the Contemplative Discovery Pathway Theory (CDPT). The CDPT is a form of positive psychology involving a mixture of cognitive-behavioral therapy, traditional psychodynamic analytic therapy and contemplative, spiritual component [7, 8].

Unlike classical group therapy, this community process had no restrictions in size, was free of charge and required no contract for attendance. The Family group is an open, dynamic and supportive process involving reflection and transformation through the sharing of personal stories (narrative). The project has increased to 22 groups with an outreach to over 300 people per week. The groups are led by a therapist or facilitator and meet for 2 hours each week. At the end of each group, the facilitator writes a praxis involving: (a) interaction, (b) analysis of overt and covert themes, (c) reflection and (d) lessons learned. These praxes are collected, filed and used for qualitative research to understand the predominant issues in the surrounding society. A thematic analysis was carried out on group sessions held in The Family program. The major themes of sessions are anger, violence, grief, relationship issues, abuse and addiction, indicating the faces of shame and the social fragmentation of the country (**Figure 2**) [9].

In addition to the well-known curative factors described so eminently by Yalom, such as information modeling, cohesion, transference, reconstitution of the early family paradigm, support, etc. [10], we found the following factors helpful in maintaining the therapeutic perspective of the group especially as it increased in size:

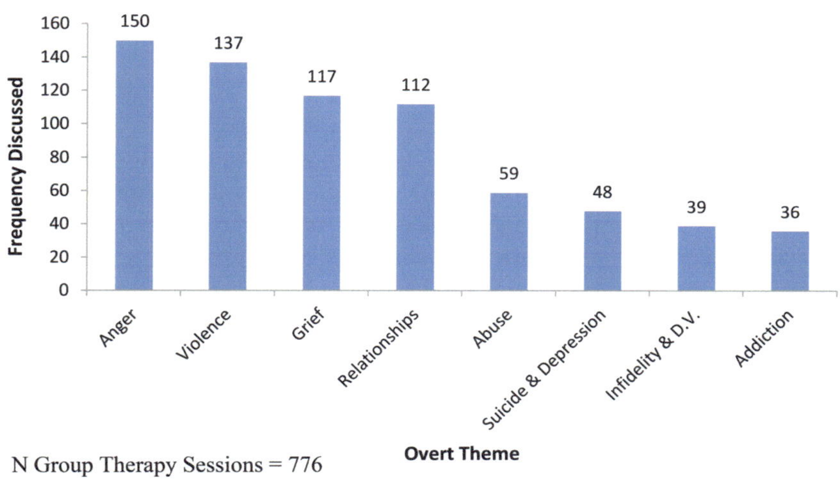

Figure 2.
Incidence of overt themes in the family sessions.

2.1 Creating a contemplative atmosphere

Each group begins with a stillness exercise involving deep breathing and imagination of following a blue light to reflect the color of the sea and sky. As the group members relax and recollect themselves, a simple prayer is made to God or a higher power. We have found the depth of the stillness exercise to be germane to the quality of the interaction in the group. Some persons, particularly in the Prison group, practice the stillness exercise throughout the week, meditating on the blue sky to experience a sense of inner peace and freedom.

2.2 Sharing our stories

a. Sharing our stories in a contemplative atmosphere is complex and requires patience and time, sometimes from 6 months to a year. Firstly, telling our story is mostly cognitive and since shame forms in the pre-cognitive phase of our development, the cognitive sharing of the story is devoid of releasing painful shame affect, which enhances positive development.

b. As the group progresses, affective sharing releases some of the painful shame feelings but often reverts back to cognitive sharing with the least distraction.

c. The deepest form of sharing our story is when we give our life with our story. Combining cognitive and affective elements, the person moves into a deeper communion with themselves and the group. Often, this results in a powerful emotional catharsis, releasing the deep shame and wounds of a lifetime.

Our experience is that it requires time, patience and understanding to wait for persons to release their stories. When a person is affectively sharing their stories with their life, it connects with the other persons in the group because that which is truly personal, is universal. Dr. Curt Thompson, referencing Dr. Daniel Siegel's work, writes, "...an important part of how people change...is through the process of telling their stories to an empathic listener. When a person tells their story and is truly heard and understood, both they and the listener undergo actual changes in their brain circuitry. They feel a greater sense of emotional and relational connection, decreased anxiety, and greater awareness of and compassion of others' suffering [11]."

In essence then, our stories, like ourselves, connect to each other, creating a vast story of human existence, healing and community.

2.3 Confidentiality

Confidentiality is important. But like trust, according to Eckhart Tolle, listening takes time for persons to become a conscious presence to each other [12]. Thus, as the healing bond develops, we tend to see ourselves in each other and feel one another's pain. Confidentiality is stressed throughout the process but group members are encouraged to examine how the discussion affects them personally. As persons mature in the group, they realize that owning their problems and working on them enables them to move toward their solution. On the other hand, denying their personal issues and focusing on gossip about others, provides little chance of resolving their problems. Our experience is that as persons recognize this, they automatically respect the confidentiality clause, mature to leaving the discussion of others in the room and focusing on their own development. When this happens in the group, the confidentiality principle is internalized and more effective.

2.4 Silence

Silence is a powerful absorber of deep negativity and shame, allowing us to heal in an atmosphere of acceptance and love. Often, the sharing of deep pain—e.g., the murder of a relative or the abuse of a child—is so painful that it can only be received at the silent level where words are inadequate and act as a distraction [13]. Opening our hearts to the evocative ability of silence releases the unconscious hurt and wounds of a lifetime. In silence, chronological time (chronos) intercepts with the fullness of time (Kairos), producing what Eliot called “the still point” of the moving world [14]. At the still point, we experience the interconnectedness of all things in the now or present. According to Tolle, the now is not only what is happening at the present, but is the united field of consciousness in which the mystery and content of our life unfurls. At the still point, we experience healing, but in a deep sense, open to the mysterious [13]. Einstein (in a speech to the German League of Human Rights), stated, “The most beautiful emotion we can experience is mysterious. It is the fundamental emotion that stands at the cradle of all true art and science. He to whom this emotion is a stranger, who can no longer wonder and stand rapt in awe, is as good as dead, a snuffed-out candle [15].”

2.5 Role-playing

Role playing of painful experiences releases deep hurt and enables participants to open up to love and healthy development. Providing new perspectives on old hurts, role-playing challenges the individual to move from being a victim to becoming a survivor. A profound and complex art, role-playing requires contemplative listening and compassion to understand the pain of another, allowing us to experience the destructive action of the perpetrator in real time. When this occurs, the group is often stunned and challenged by the pathos of the situation resulting in a powerful catharsis releasing deep hurt and pain [13].

2.6 Centering

In the process of centering, we invite the person sharing their pain to come to the center of the group where they are joined by the therapist and other participants who identify with their situation. As a result, the group becomes two concentric groups, the inner being the pain sharers and the outer the pain bearers. As the painful story is released, a powerful catharsis results, not only releasing the pain of the victim, but enabling others to express their pain as well. The catharsis is followed by a deep sense of reverential silence, reflection and understanding. At this point, the group is extremely cohesive and persons have difficulty in leaving [13].

2.7 Social activities

Social activities—for example a birthday celebration, a hospital visitation, picnic or holiday party—are extremely important and have a powerful healing effect on the group. A recurring observation is that often a very challenged person is deeply encouraged by visiting or celebrating with another hurt person. A number of persons have described how the social activity helped them to release their pain and gave them courage to face the future [13].

2.8 Singing

Singing is a powerful unifying force in the group, calming the intense emotional experience of anger, grief and revenge. The Negro Spirituals have proved particularly helpful. For example,

"Sometimes I feel like a motherless child, a long, long way from home. Sometimes I feel like a fatherless child, a long way from home."

The resonance of these words has a powerful effect on the group as they are reminded of home being a place where they felt safe and at peace. As the spiritual is sung, tears stream down the faces of many participants as they release their deep hurt and shame. At the end of the song the silence absorbs the pain and longing so prevalent in the group. Another example of the power of song was when a Family member shared the painful story of being at her sister's death bed and how her faith enabled her to give her sister hope. At this point of sadness, one of the facilitators sang the song "His Eye is on the Sparrow, and I know He cares for me." The group experienced a powerful sense of oneness and healing. At the end of our Family sessions, we hold hands and sing the song "Bind Us Together in Love." As the group separates, this provides a sense of connection and a continuation of the healing effect of the group even after the session is terminated [13].

2.9 Humor

The heart with deep pain responds to humor. However, to be effective, the humor must be intimately connected to the process while expressing the opposite. The juxtaposition of these two realities release affect while producing a transcendent joviality. For example, the Bahamas has a Christian cultural orientation. It is not uncommon for people in the group to assure each other by saying "God will be there for you." At that point, the facilitator may tell a story about the mother who told Johnny to get the broom from outside while it was dark. Johnny replied, "Mummy, I'm afraid of the dark." Mother said "Johnny, don't be afraid of the dark. God is everywhere." Taking her literally, Johnny opens the door and shouts into the darkness "God, since you're everywhere, can you please pass me the broom?" Despite the sadness, the group breaks into laughter, releasing hurt and shame. Humor allows people to see themselves in perspective and not take themselves too seriously while releasing them, if only temporarily, from their hurt and pain [13].

2.10 Spiritual teaching

At the end of the group when people are overwhelmed by the pathos and suffering of others, a psycho-spiritual teaching provides a sense of calm, encouragement and hope. Examples of such spiritual teachings that have been used effectively include: loving when the dream of love has shattered (the Jewish story of Ruth and Naomi), facing the painful giants in our life (the story of David and Goliath) and forgiveness (the story of the prodigal son, particularly as portrayed in Rembrandt's painting). We also used stories involving Bahamian folklore and parables. For example "you can break one stick but it's hard to break ten" or "loose goat doesn't know how tied goat feels" [13].

2.11 Insights from neuroscience

Neuroscience offers novel ways to think about the benefits of The Family. In his book "Brainstorm," Siegel claims that we interact with the world in two views of reality: the physical world of objects and mindsight. Sadly, modern life has become more dependent on physical sight than recognizing the importance of our mind connection. This is challenging because without the mind connection, people can treat others without respect or compassion.

The Family Project is based on mindsight where we help individuals to develop their internal world to relate more effectively to themselves and others. According to Siegel, focusing our mind on multiple interactions—for example, telling our stories, listening, singing, meditation, social action, etc.—helps us build new circuits in our brain enabling us to adapt creatively to new experiences while increasing our health and developing harmonious relationships. Mindsight includes three fundamental skills: insight, empathy and integration. Insight is our ability to appreciate our inner mental life, helping us to understand the present, past and future. When we reflect on things going on inside of us, we develop mindsight mapping of the brain, activating our pre-frontal circuits where the inner and interpersonal experiences are coordinated and balanced. Empathy is the ability to sense the inner life of another person, enabling us to see them from our perspective and imagine what it is like to walk in their shoes. The gateway to compassion and kindness, empathy is the key to social intelligence, allowing us to understand the intention and needs of others. In this light, relationships can be defined as the sharing of energy and information between persons. Insight and empathy cultivates integration empowering us to coordinate our relationships with each other. Sadly, when integration is blocked, chaos results in our internal and external relationships, developing a powerful rigidity which destroys individual and community development. These neuroscientific insights validate the effect of The Family where people share their stories of pain and shame in a contemplative environment, creating mindsight (insight, empathy and integration) in the participants leading to coordination, balance and self-regulation [13, 16].

3. Contemplative Discovery Pathway Theory

A developmental model, the CDPT postulates that the self follows the step-wise path from the natural self at birth to the shame self and its antithesis, the addictive shame false self, leading to the development of the authentic self (**Figures 3–6**) [7]. According to the Judeo Christian tradition, human beings are made in the image of God, and are hard wired to seek unconditional love. At birth we have three basic instinctual needs, (a) safety (survival/security), (b) connection (affirmation and esteem) and (c) empowerment (power and control) [17]. These three dimensions are powerful sources of energy, which interact with each other as a child struggles to develop basic trust making the natural self-vulnerable, fragile and extremely dependent on the support of others [13].

According to Heinz Kohut, these instinctual needs form the basis of our early self-object transference. Survival security relates to the mirror transference leading to the sense of affirmation. The affection/esteem leads to the twin-ship transference, resulting in the development of empathy and community. Power/control leads to the idealized transference giving rise to respect, honor and worship [18].

The basic instinctual needs are also the substance of which our dreams are made. When a dream shatters, a lie is born. For example, when the dream of safety shatters, creating an abandonment shame schema, the person believes the lie "I am hopeless. No one wants me and I'm not enough." When the dream of connection is shattered, creating the rejection shame schema, the lie develops "No one wants me. I am unlovable. I will never have a relationship." When the dream of empowerment shatters, creating the humiliation shame schema, the lies develop "I am helpless. I am a failure. I can't cope." These lies, if not confronted, can become delusions which are fixed false beliefs unalterable to argument and lead a person's life to destruction. The fact is, it is easier to confront reality than to conquer a lie.

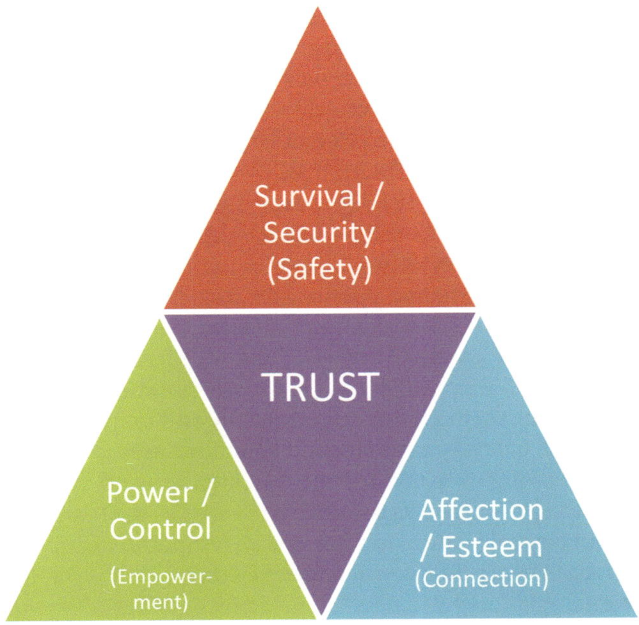

Figure 3.
The natural self.

Figure 4.
The shame self.

Life is wounded and we all experience variations of hurt leading to development of SHAME (Self Hatred Aimed at ME) involving feelings of abandonment, rejection and humiliation. Deeply painful to the human psyche, shame is compensated for by the development of the defensive, addictive, shame false self, involving self-absorption, self-gratification and control. The false self is illusory, made up of many layers and enhances negative programs for happiness which hijack the

Figure 5.
The shame false self.

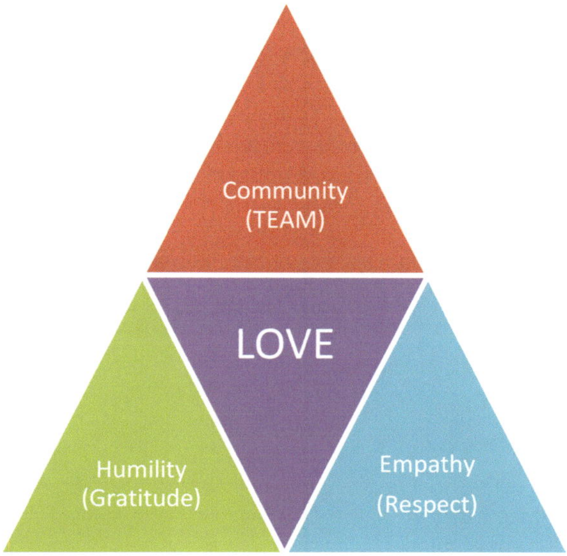

Figure 6.
The authentic self.

meaning and purpose of our lives, causing us to wander aimlessly in the wilderness of fear and anger [13]. This makes the false self what we call "the Bermuda Triangle of the soul." It is a perverse rescuer, promising hope but delivering destruction. If the lies from the shattering of the dreams of safety, connection and empowerment are not neutralized, they culminate in the complexity of the development of the false self. In The Family, the loving support of the group allows members to share their stories. As they surrender the grief and shame of their pain, they release their negativity and destructiveness and embrace the positive healing emotions of love and support. As a result, the shame false self melts away, giving rise to Discovery of the Authentic Gracious Self characterized by love, community, humility and gratitude.

4. The Evil Violence Tunnel

When a person is deeply shamed and is further hurt or provoked, they develop murderous rage triggering the Evil Violence Tunnel (**Figure** 7) [19]. The Evil Violence Tunnel has six stages:

1. Cognitive restriction, in which the person feels trapped and their rage is directed toward the person shaming them (perpetrator).

2. Physiological arousal—the heart rate and pulse rate rises, the person sweats profusely and often their I.Q. drops, causing them to act irresponsibly and not in keeping with their normal intelligent mode of function.

3. Emotional numbness—at this stage, the person suffers from a form of alexithemia, dumbs down emotionally and is unable to feel empathically with the other person. They may have a cognitive sense of how the victim feels but are unable to identify with the feelings. As a result, they are totally destructive and unaware of the pain of the victim. For example, a gentleman continued stabbing a lady, who he claimed shamed him by cheating on him. When asked why he continued to stab her, he replied "I wanted her to feel what I was feeling." But when challenged about what he was feeling, he said "I don't know."

4. Negative energy—persons have shared with us that at this stage, they are flooded with negative emotions and energy and become totally destructive.

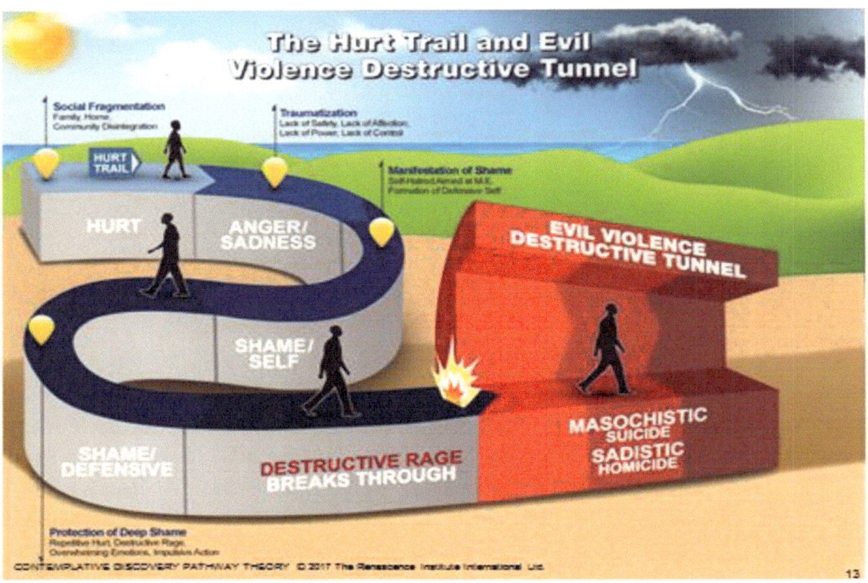

Figure 7.
The evil violence tunnel.

5. Ethical fragmentation—regardless of the person's moral, ethical or religious background, at this point, their anger is so intense, their values collapse and they become vicious to themselves or others.

6. Compulsive, repetitive, destructive action—this destructive action may be addressed to the person themselves, leading to self-injury or suicide or it may be projected onto another person, leading to harming them or even homicide.

We allowed inmates in the local prison to examine our description of this phenomenon and give us their perspective. The inmates agreed with the stages but did not like the psychological terminology. As a result, they replaced it with their own:

1. Fixation

2. Being psyched

3. Dumbing down to hurt and destroy

4. Overwhelmed by the devil

5. Nothing good can happen now

6. Total destruction against the self or the other

The Evil Violence Tunnel is triggered by various types of provocation and enhanced by the use of alcohol or drugs. We have found that after a person has been destructive, they go through a time of quiet and relaxation before they recognize the full tragedy of what has occurred. This may be due to intoxication or emotional flooding.

5. The false self and dualistic thinking

The false self, unlike our authentic self, involves dualistic thinking where we separate our adequate side from our shame self. This enhances the process of scapegoating to allow the false self to maintain control. According to René Girard, "when human beings cannot, or dare not, take out their anger on the thing (or person) that caused it, they unconsciously search for substitutes, and more often than not, they find them [20]." In sadistic scapegoating, we split off the shame self and project it on to the other person, who is blamed and judged as inferior, making the perpetrator feel more self-righteous or superior. In masochistic scapegoating, we split off our adequate self, leaving us a victim with a deeper sense of shame or what may be called a martyr-like syndrome, where we feel totally inadequate, cry "poor me" and give our power away to others because we see them as superior.

This is the opposite of our authentic true self, whose thinking is non-dualistic, is not involved in splitting and always presents the adequate and shame self together. In our true self, we talk about our strengths but accept our weaknesses because they cannot be divorced from each other.

6. Discovery (resocialization)

"Each person's life is a challenging journey from being a victim of their shame and False Self based in fear and anger to experience the Discovery of the glorious freedom of their True Authentic Self based in love, gratitude and meaningful community" (Dr. David Allen).

How do we make the transition from the elusive, victimizing, inner critic of our Shame false self based in fear to discover the freedom of our authentic self based in love and gratitude? The story of the Velveteen rabbit says it all. In this story, the Velveteen rabbit is the newest toy to be added to the young boy's toy barn. Looking around, the Velveteen rabbit sees the shining tin soldiers, the proud lion and the old skin horse with his tail torn off and his fur worn away. Feeling shy, alone and lost, the old skin horse, who had been in the boy's toy barn for many years, tells the Velveteen rabbit he needs to become real. Amazed, the Velveteen rabbit asked the skin horse, "What does it mean to become real?" The old skin horse, speaking from his years of experience and wisdom, tells the Velveteen rabbit, "You only become real when someone really loves you!" [13].

In The Family, people experience an atmosphere of loving concern and non-judgment as they share their painful stories releasing their hurt and shame [13]. As a result, the heart or psyche like a sponge is emptied of the hurt and shame, allowing them to embrace the love in the group. Breaking through the negativity of our shame false self, we face the fear and anger of our shame self involving abandonment, rejection and humiliation. As we confront our shame self and release our painful feelings, we experience the discovery of our true self based in love, gratitude and healing community. Discovery is not an event but a process requiring continual commitment to confront the pain of our shame and release it through the catharsis of grieving and surrender. As we become more open to love, The Family provides an opportunity to practice it and see it demonstrated in ourselves and other persons in the group. In so doing, we make the perceptual shift from fear and shame to the discovery of love and compassion. We can actually see this happen when once angry and hurt people release their shame and become healers in the group. It is important to note, however, that because of the woundedness of life, we will tend to fall back from our true self to our shame false self. But we do not stay there because the vision of love in our heart moves us toward our true self and our potential rather than being addicted or stuck at the limitations of our false self. Discovery is a process of resocialization where our self-esteem and solidarity increases as we become authentic and move in love to create healing community. According to Marcel Proust, "The real voyage of discovery consists not in seeking new landscapes, but in having new eyes" [21].

7. Research

Although there was good testimonial evidence of resocialization (see Case Vignettes), we received a grant to carry out a Pilot, quantitative study. Because there was no suitable resocialization instrument, a combination of nine international scales (namely the Beck Depression Inventory, Buss-Durkee Hostility-Guilt Inventory, Gratitude Questionnaire, Hope Scale, Self-Deception Questionnaire, Internalized Shame Scale, Satisfaction with life Scale, Spiritual Well-Being Scale and Transgression-Related Interpersonal Motivations Inventory (TRIM-18)) was used to test participants. Participants also completed a baseline questionnaire to ascertain their impression before The Family. They were studied in two cohorts at 6 month intervals of persons who had been in The Family for over a year or more [13].

Results showed that persons in The Family a year or more had a decrease in anger (**Figure 8**), depression, violence, revenge, loneliness and abusive relationships (**Figure 9**). They also reported an increase in self-esteem, benevolence and contentedness with life with trends toward increases in forgiveness and gratitude (**Figure 10**) [8, 13].

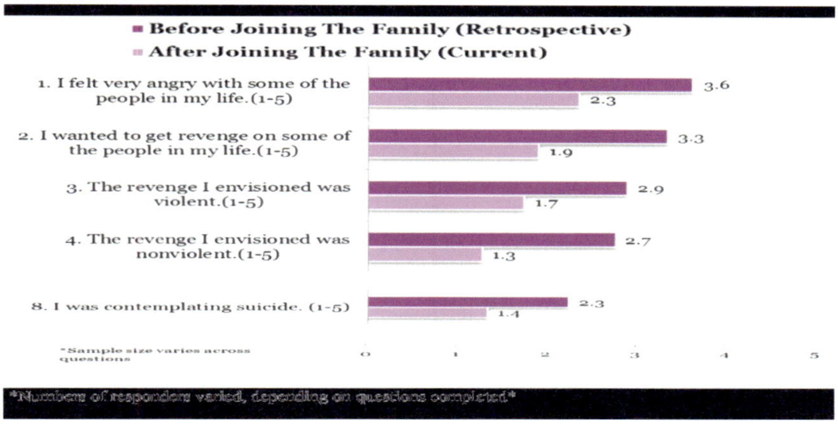

Figure 8.
Participants indicated that after joining the family, they felt significantly less anger toward others (t = −2.83, p = 0.0142, Cohen's d = −0.756). They also showed significantly decreased desire for vengeance (t = −3.32, p = 0.0061, Cohen's d = −0.922), and experienced significantly fewer thoughts of both violent and nonviolent revenge (t = −2.28, p = 0.0437, Cohen's d = −0.658).

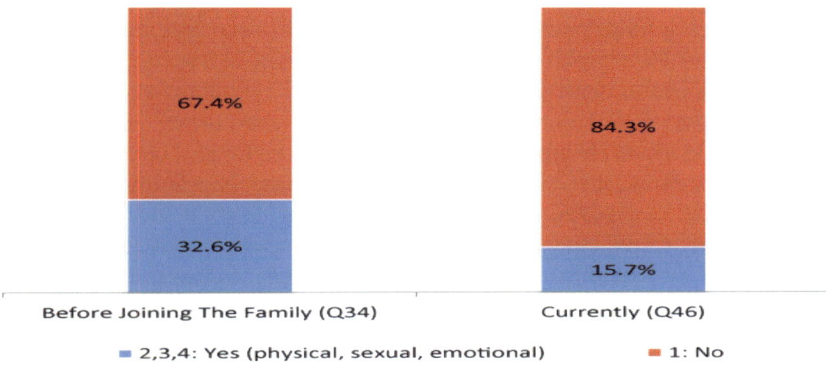

Figure 9.
Q34 of the questionnaire asked "Before joining the Family, were you in an abusive relationship?" 32.6% of participants indicated "yes," 67.4% indicated "no." Q46 of the questionnaire asked "Are you currently in an abusive relationship?" 15.7% indicated "yes," 84.3% indicated "no."

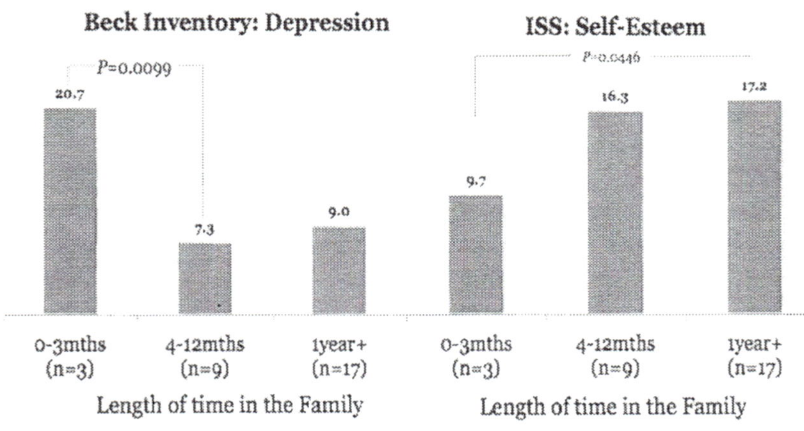

Figure 10.
Significant areas of change with increased time in the family.

As a result we received a grant from the Templeton World Charity Foundation, to (a) continue the research and expand The Family Project, (b) develop an international resocialization instrument (Allen Resocialization Scale) and (c) create a program to train lay persons as therapist facilitators [13]. We have completed this grant and the results validate those of the pilot study.

8. A resocialization intervention model in the prison

The Family group therapy program was implemented in the Bahamas Department of Corrections over four (4) years ago. Inmates who are in a pre-release program are allowed to attend the sessions. Each week, three trained therapists meet with a group of inmates for 90 minutes. There are two group sessions, one for the male inmates and another for the females. Three principles govern the sessions: confidentiality, non-judgmental approach and free expression. Group members are empowered when they share their stories. Taking ownership of the group, they renamed it the "Free Your Mind Group." Anger was one of the most prominent themes in the sessions. The therapists worked through the inmates' anger by exploring the underlying fears and hurts involved. Stories and myths were also used by the therapists to connect with the inmates. An example of one of the stories used is the Slave Myth. In this myth, a slave was tied to a stake. While chained, he would look into the distance and admire the verdant mountains. He often dreamed of what it would be like to be free. One night, an angel broke his chain. Realizing what had happened, he ran toward the mountains to seize his freedom. Unfortunately, he began to fear the unknown. He started to worry about his survival. He looked back at his broken chain and decided to reattach it to himself. In his mind, he figured that being enslaved provided him with the necessities of life, such as food, drink, etc. He walked around his stake for the rest of his life. Although his external chains were broken, the internal chains around his heart were still intact. This particular myth resonated with the inmates and a discussion about physical and mental freedom ensued. The reality that one could be physically free but mentally imprisoned began to set in. At this moment, the therapists stressed that it was The Family's mission to break the internal chains around their hearts and assist them in developing their inner life.

The development of trust was another issue initially faced by the therapists. Despite the inmates being skeptical of them, they continued to provide consistency, stability and predictability. In the inception of the group, one of the original therapists was Mr. André Chappelle who was a resocialized drug addict. Mr. Chappelle had been incarcerated five times so the inmates were quite familiar with him. In fact, the miracle of his transformation became a catalyst of hope for them. They told him "you give us hope. If you can change your life, we can also."

A thematic analysis carried out on 109 of the group sessions conducted in the prison indicated that the four most common themes of the discussions were violence, anger, revenge and addiction. The inmates indicated that anger fuels their violent acts. Revenge is a justification for violence and addiction to external substances helps them cope. According to one of the inmates "when you kill for the first time, you feel sick and can't stop thinking about it. You feel like you're going crazy. After a while, you get used to it, get drunk and high and you feel numb" [22]. Another inmate described the depth of his anger when he disclosed:

"I hate people. I can't trust them because they hurt me badly. My mother abandoned me at 8 years old, went to the U.S. and had another family. My father also abandoned me and my grandmother raised me. The rest of my family members and neighbors scorned me. My daughter is my only love but sadly I've abandoned her and I hate myself because I've done to her what was done to me" [22].

A female inmate shared her experience of being in the Evil Violence Tunnel:

"I was raised by my grandmother and I knew all kinds of abuse growing up. When I was in my late 20's I was a single mother with a good enough job at a hotel. I started dating this [man] because I wanted to play him. I wanted to make him believe I was carrying his child so he could take care of me and my children. As time went by, he started to become more and more violent and I started to hate him deeply. I even told him the child was not his. One day I was back from work and I was combing my hair while he was screaming at me, calling me names and threatening to rape me one more time. Suddenly, I attacked him with the comb in my hand. To my horror, the metal comb went all the way to his skull. The blood came pouring out and he died instantly. I still remember seeing my son cleaning the blood on the floor with the mop. I was in the newspaper and felt ashamed. I attempted suicide by setting the prison cell on fire. I am happy I survived because I realize now that my children and my mother are waiting for me to get out. I have people I love and this keeps me going" [22].

There are signs of resocialization in the participants. One inmate, imprisoned for 25 years, is running a Toastmaster's program to assist other inmates who are interested in learning the art of public speaking. The inmates now delay gratification and have better impulse control. They have also developed better conflict resolution skills and now have more effective communication. Even more so, they are now able to express vulnerability by sharing intimate, personal and emotional stories with the group [22].

9. Case vignettes

The names used in these vignettes are fictitious to conceal the identity of The Family participants.

9.1 Abuse

When Doreen came to The Family she was broken and deeply hurt. Incested and abused by her father for many years, her life was threatened if she ever revealed the family secret. Seeking to escape her abusive family she married a man who at first seemed loving but eventually became verbally and physically abusive, threatening to kill her numerous times. Distraught and depressed, Doreen became suicidal and was referred to The Family. When she was ready to share her story, Doreen was invited to come to the center of the group supported by therapists and persons who identified with her pain. After a while, Doreen was able to verbalize her pain, exploding into a powerful catharsis screaming at the top of her voice for 3 minutes or more, releasing the shame of a lifetime. This was followed by a powerful silence in the group where persons prayed and others meditated or cried. After the catharsis, persons in the group comforted and encouraged Doreen. Having been in The Family group for 5 years, Doreen is a changed person. She is a healer who has helped many persons face and work through their painful experiences of abuse. Recently receiving a promotion at work, she was one of the first graduates of the therapist facilitator training program [13].

9.2 The terror of poverty and social deprivation

Rejected by his family, George left home at 13 years old to fend for himself on the streets. Living on the beach and in abandoned buildings, George hustled daily to make ends meet. He was severely abused—physically and sexually. Later on George was shot in his face and side and admitted to hospital. On the third day of his hospitalization, the person who shot George was also shot. Admitted to the same hospital, he was placed two beds away from George. Angry and filled with revenge George wanted him dead. The next day George's gang came to the hospital seeking to kill the person who shot George. They begged George to identify the shooter, but George refused. Instead, he surrendered his feelings of revenge and prayed for a better life. After release from hospital, George's life became worse. He lived in a tomb in one of the graveyards and was eventually referred to The Family Project. Facing a loss of confidence in himself, George was shy, ashamed and unable to speak. The group was very receptive and showered him with love, giving him odd jobs, clothes, food and money. After a number of sessions, George began to speak freely and socialize with the participants in the group. A few months later, he shared that when he first came to The Family, he felt his life was hopeless. He said he is now determined to live again because of the love he found in our sessions. George is still in The Family, has a job and volunteers in The Family basketball outreach program to marginalized youth [13].

9.3 Murder

The Family has had many experiences working with persons who suffered the murder of a loved one. One of the most outstanding experiences is that of Mrs. Jones who had been a member of The Family for about a year. She had previously brought her young daughter to The Family for help. One evening, I received a call at 11:00 pm that her daughter was shot and killed in the living room. Visiting the family was a painful and horrific experience as the details of the murder were explained. Mrs. Jones, although distraught and grieving, shared that because of her work in The Family, she wanted to work toward forgiveness rather than revenge. This was difficult because she was being encouraged by other family members and neighbors to seek revenge. This is not unusual because revenge is the normal reaction for these types of incidents in marginalized neighborhoods. Returning to The Family meetings, Mrs. Jones worked on expressing her grief. At times she would scream at the top of her voice and describe how she would go to the graveyard at 3:00 am and cry out over her daughter's body. Most interesting, Mrs. Jones shared that the evening before her daughter was murdered, they watched a film "I Spit on Your Grave," in which there is a scene where a rape victim says "Vengeance is mine, says the Lord, and I will repay." According to Mrs. Jones, her daughter stopped the film three times, emphasizing these words. Mrs. Jones' question to The Family group was whether her daughter knew something that she did not know. Her journey toward forgiveness was not an easy one but as she worked in The Family week after week, expressing her grief and sorrow, eventually she came to a point where she was able to forgive the killer of her daughter.

Our experience in The Family is that forgiveness is a long road, especially because deep hurts, like murder, are multi-dimensional. Even though Mrs. Jones came out on the side of forgiveness, there are certain periods of time when a development happens in her neighborhood or family and she becomes angry and says to me "Dr. Allen, I want to buy a gun." But we listen quietly, allowing her to express her anger, hurt and especially her shame. She returns to the desire to forgive rather than seek revenge. It has been two and half years now, and she is still on the journey to forgiveness, with the periodic ups and downs of drifting into revengeful thoughts.

9.4 Addiction

The Family groupgreat interest in the process of sharing has been most affected by André Chappelle, who I initially treated for cocaine addiction when he was 15 years old. Although he had flights into sobriety, he would regress and eventually became homeless, indigent and a vagrant. On the street for over 20 years, he had a reputation of being polite and kind. For example, he tutored students at the College of the Bahamas and was very helpful to ladies whose vehicles would break down. On Christmas morning, 2009, at 2:00 am, he described an intense feeling of loneliness and despair as his addictive, destructive lifestyle haunted him. Falling to his knees, he cried out for help. This eventually led to him going to the family's lawyer, who helped him clear his criminal record and travel to the U.S. to visit his sister. Returning to Nassau, he came to The Family group and expressed great interest in the process of sharing his personal story. He read all the published papers of The Family, studied to become a facilitator, and became my right-hand person in the program. As the addiction lifted, he was able to, in his own words, "squeeze the sponge of his heart to release the hurt and shame and make space for love" from the group, the people around him and of course his early religious faith. Eventually the love he had for a young lady in the eighth grade returned and they were married. He worked very closely with me and became perhaps the best interpreter of the CDPT. Sadly, in 2016, he developed an inoperable colon carcinoma. I walked with him to the very end as he shared his story of life but also the challenge of death. His dying words were "The Family is special because there are not many places in society where people can walk off the street, squeeze the hurt and shame out of the sponge of their heart by sharing their story and experience the discovery of the freedom of becoming authentic."

10. Conclusion

The Family has become a healing balm for many in the Bahamian community. In some sense, it is the grieving center for persons who have undergone serious losses of relatives through murder and violent crime. It is a place where people meet others who have suffered the trauma of abuse and shame which has held them captive all their lives. It is very common to hear the shout of "you too?" or "me too," indicating a harmonious connection among traumatic experiences in the group that liberates people to release their shame and discover the freedom to be essentially who they are. More than that, The Family is a place for dialog. As societies around the world become more polarized, there is an urgent need for creative dialog between races, different socioeconomic groups, political groups, law enforcement and community, etc. The fact is that simply sharing our stories illustrates The Family mantra "jaw jaw stops war war."

Acknowledgements

This work was funded by a grant from the Templeton World Charity Foundation.

Conflicts of interest

None of the authors have any conflicts of interest.

Author details

David F. Allen*, Keva Bethell, Marie Allen-Carroll and Flavia D'Alessandro
Allen Institute of Research and Training, Nassau, Bahamas

*Address all correspondence to: dfallen43@gmail.com

References

[1] Jekel JF, Allen DF, Podlewski H, Clarke N, Dean-Patterson S, Cartwright P. Epidemic free-base cocaine abuse. Case study from the Bahamas. Lancet. 1986;**1**(8479):459-462

[2] Shaw C, McKay H. Juvenile Delinquency and Urban Areas. Chicago, IL: University of Chicago Press; 1942

[3] Arrigo B, Takahashi Y. Recommunalization of the disenfranchised: A theoretical and critical criminological inquiry. Theoretical Criminology. 2006;**10**(3):307-336

[4] Liaudinskien G. Resocialization barriers of juvenile delinquents. Social Science. 2005;**47**(1):41-48

[5] Skiecevicius P, Leliugiene I. Empowering partnership as resocialization form of juveniles subject to delinquency: Findings of empirical research. Socialiniai Mokslai. 2012;**75**(1):30-40

[6] Allen DF. Shame: The Human Nemesis. Washington, D.C.: Eleuthera Publications; 2010

[7] Allen D, Mayo M, Allen-Carroll M, Manganello J, Allen VS. Cultivating gratitude: Contemplative discovery pathway theory applied to group therapy in the Bahamas. Journal of Trauma & Treatment. 2014;**3**(3):197

[8] Allen D, Allen-Carroll M, Allen V, Bethell K, Manganello J. Community resocialization via instillation of family values through a novel group therapy approach: A pilot study. Journal of Psychotherapy Integration. 2015;**25**(4):289-298

[9] Bethell K, Allen D, Allen-Carroll M. Using a supportive community group process to cope with the trauma of social fragmentation and promote resocialization in the Bahamas. Emergency Medicine: Open Access. 2015;**5**(2):244

[10] Yalom I. The Theory and Practice of Group Psychotherapy. New York: Basic Books; 1970

[11] Thompson C. Anatomy of the Soul. Carol Stream: Tyndale House Publishers; 2010

[12] Tolle E. Stillness Speaks. Novato: New World Library; 2003

[13] Allen DF, Bethell K, Allen-Carroll M. A resocialization intervention model: The family: People helping people project. Clinical Case Reports and Reviews. 2016;**2**(7):491-495

[14] Eliot TS. Collected Poems (1909-1962). New York: Harcourt, Brace & World; 1963

[15] Gookin J. Wilderness Wisdom Quotes for Inspirational Explorations. Mechanicsburg: Stackpole Books; 2003

[16] Siegel D. Brainstorm. New York, NY: Penguin Press; 2013

[17] Keating T. Open Mind Open Heart: The Contemplative Dimension of the Gospel. New York: The Continuum International Publishing Group Inc; 1986

[18] Kohut H. How Does Analysis Cure? Chicago: University of Chicago Press; 1984

[19] Allen D, Bethell K, Allen-Carroll M. Anger and social fragmentation: The evil violence tunnel. Journal of Psychotherapy Integration. 2016;**27**(1):79-92

[20] Girard R. The One by Whom Scandal Comes. East Lansing: Michigan State University Press; 2014

[21] Proust M. In Search of Lost Time. France: Grasset and Gallimard; 1913

[22] Allen D, D'Alessandro M, Bethell K. A resocialization intervention model in the prison—The family: People helping people project. Sociology International Journal. 2017;**1**(4)